HARMONIC MATRICES®
FOR GUITAR AND OTHER INSTRUMENTS

William A. Cronkrite

ARCHWAY
PUBLISHING

Archway Publishing books may be ordered through booksellers or by contacting:

Archway Publishing
1663 Liberty Drive
Bloomington, IN 47403
www.archwaypublishing.com
844-669-3957

ISBN: 978-1-6657-0583-7 (sc)
ISBN: 978-1-6657-0584-4 (e)

Library of Congress Control Number: 2021908066

Print information available on the last page.

Archway Publishing rev. date: 08/20/2021

I would like to dedicate this work to my father William Richard Cronkrite, 5/5/1930 – 1/29/2021. He was truly one of the unsung heroes of this country. Not only was he a naval veteran of the Korean War but also a Staff Scientist for Hercules Aerospace Division and the engineer responsible for the Space Shuttle SRB mandrels as well as several other significant rockets used by the United States of America – a proverbial "rocket scientist" and one of the most humble human beings I have ever known. May he rest in peace.

I would like to especially thank Bill Burraston for an amazing cover design and Howard Jensen for assisting me with my first edit. Finally, I would like to thank Archway Publishing for assisting me with the publication of this book. Their patience and assistance throughout this process has been amazing. Thank-you

VOLUME 1 TABLE OF CONTENTS

INTRODUCTION

This text describes a unique methodology to facilitate understanding how to evaluate and analyze a piece of music or portions of a piece of music in terms of "diatonic harmony". This is accomplished by the use of harmonic matrices which show all of the chords gernerated by a particular scale as well as all of the modes generated by that scale. Diatonic harmony is a system of chords that pertains to or is derived from a scale. Many pieces of music are written in a single key. Some pieces are "chromatic", "atonal", or "polytonal". These are terms used to describe music utilizing the twelve tone scale, no particular scale or key, or multiple scales or keys, respectively. Apart from chromatic and atonal music, many pieces can be viewed as polytonal - having more than one key or key center. Polytonal pieces can be approached from a "diatonic" perspective. That is, the music can be broken up into parts, each having their own key center.

The art of improvisation is greatly facilitated by knowing the scales and how to apply them to a given chord progression. The scale forms for the guitar presented in this text follow the "sweeping pattern" format as opposed to the "traditional" forms. That is , all scale forms will employ a three note per string format over position. Most of the scales shown can be found in every key in "THE GUITAR GRIMOIRE - SCALES & MODES". Additionally, "THE GUITAR GRIMOIRE - CHORDS & VOICINGS" shows effectively what scales can be "generated" by a given chord. In improvising over a set of changes (chords in succession) it is not always practical to change scales each time the chord changes. Indeed, the selection of an appropriate scale is usually dependent on the chord progression, or the chords that preceed and follow a given chord, in a key.

The harmonic matrices shown in this text are seven by twelve grids of chords. The seven columns represent a "modal" progression of the scale. A numerical naming convention is used throughout the text regardless of the type of scale. The twelve rows list the basic triad followed by all of the commonly used extensions and variations of the chord in a specific order . Organized this way, the matrices show all the possible chords that would be in a chord progression belonging to a particular key center or scale.

Of the chord forms shown, it should be noted that no particular rules associated with voice leading, doubling, or spacing are observed. These choices are often a matter of preference or context. Chord forms are selected arbitrarily with the common forms taking precedence. Chord forms for the upper extensions, namely the eleventh and thirteenth, utilize most or all of the pitches in the scale or key, making the notes in those chords identical from mode to mode. Therefore, a root movement scenario is employed for the purpose of establishing tonal differentiation. Additionally, since the guitar can only utilize six pitches, some pitches are omitted in the chord forms shown.

The arpeggio options included represent all of the pitches for the chord within the range of the sweeping pattern and are offered as melodic alternatives. The reader should make some effort to determine the arpeggios in the other regions of the neck. No fingerings are included in this text since these often are a matter of personal choice for position.

The harmonic matrices serve as a reference to the systems of diatonic harmony generated for each key center, and list all of the chord extensions that exist in that key. They are a means of readily determining the scale(s) generated by a chord progression used in improvisation. Furthermore, they serve as a compositional tool to define all of the chord "colors" in a particular key.

It is the author's sincere hope that you find the information in this text useful and beneficial in the creation of your own music.

DIATONIC HARMONY - Basic Theory

Before discussing the specifics associated with chord construction and diatonic harmony, a review of "basic theory" is necessary. It is assumed that the reader can already read music and have an understanding of how the major scale is constructed. Additionally, a knowledge of the key signatures and the circle of fifths is important to understand chord construction.

To begin with, the octave in music represents a 2:1 frequency ratio. In other words, if a certain pitch is 440 cycles per second, the next octave up would be 880 cycles per second. In western cultures, the octave is divided into twelve parts, equidistant from one another in terms of their frequency ratio. This is known as a "twelve-tone equal temperament" or simply as 12-TET. There are other systems of tuning which divide the octave differently, such as the 5-TET, 7-TET, 31-TET, etc. The construction of the guitar neck is representative of the 12-TET system of tuning. From the nut (open string) to the octave there are 12 frets. The twelfth fret usually has two position markers, as opposed to just one. Each fret, or division of the octave represents one half step in music, which is our basic unit of measurement. Two half steps equals one whole step.

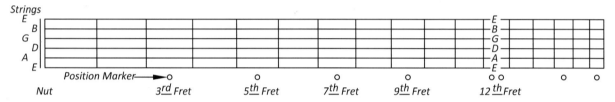

In western cultures, the musical alphabet consists of the seven natural notes - A, B, C, D, E, F, & G. There is 1 whole step between successive natural notes except 1/2 step between B & C and E & F. A sharp is used to raise the pitch value by one half step and a flat is used to decrease a pitch value by one half step. A sequence of sharps or flats also represent the pitches in between the natural notes with one step between them. Thus, the notes on the fretboard of the guitar are as follows:

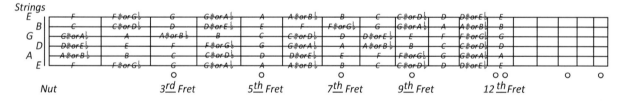

F sharp and G flat are an example of the same pitch being spelled differently. The two spellings are known as "enharmonic equivalents".

The study of diatonic harmony must begin with an understanding of intervals. "Interval" is the term used to describe the frequency distance between two pitches. The rules for naming the intervals are derived from the intervals of the major scales. Using the "C" Major scale, the basic intervals are as follows:

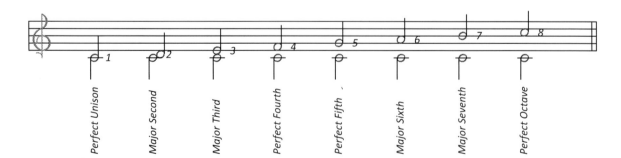

2

Basic theory - continued

Note that the interval is named by counting the lines and spaces from the first note, including the line or space that the first note is on. Intervals that utilize pitches that are not contained in the major scale are named according to the following rules:

1. A major interval (distance) reduced in size by a 1/2 step is a minor interval. C to E is a major third - C to E flat is a minor third.
2. A perfect interval reduced by a 1/2 step is a diminished interval. C to G is a perfect fifth - C to G flat is a diminished fifth.
3. A minor interval reduced by a 1/2 step is a diminished interval.
4. When either a major interval or a perfect interval is increased by a 1/2 step the resulting interval is called augmented. C to E is a major third - C to E sharp is an augmented third. C to F is a perfect fourth - C to F sharp is an augmented fourth.
5. Intervals are judged with reference to the key signature of the lowest pitch in the interval. While the interval C to E is a major third, E up to C is a minor sixth since C is sharped in the key of E. The interval of E down to C would also be a major third.
6. Intervals are named by their spelling, not their sound. While C to F sharp is an augmented fourth and C to G flat is a diminished fifth. Even though F sharp and G flat are enharmonic equivalents (the same pitch), the correct naming of the interval, C to G flat is a diminished fifth, not an augmented fourth.

CHORD CONSTRUCTION

A chord, by definition, is created by sounding three or more different pitches simultaneously. The system of harmony, or chord construction, most often employed by music of western cultures, is called tertiary (tertiary meaning three) harmony. Tertiary harmony means the chords are constructed from the scales by stacking thirds. There is another form of harmony called quartal harmony which bases chord construction on the interval of a fourth. Quartal harmony is not addressed in this text. Additionally, modern power chords are two note "broken chords" or simply intervals.

The first chords covered in this text are "triads" or basic three note chords. Triads are constructed by stacking thirds over each note in a scale utilizing only the notes in that scale. This is, by definition, diatonic harmony. Following is the C major scale - harmonized by constructing triads over each scale degree.

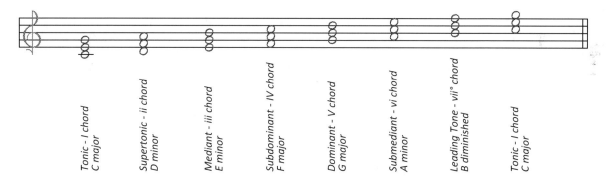

Tonic - I chord
C major

Supertonic - ii chord
D minor

Mediant - iii chord
E minor

Subdominant - IV chord
F major

Dominant - V chord
G major

Submediant - vi chord
A minor

Leading Tone - vii° chord
B diminished

Tonic - I chord
C major

Each chord in the key of C contains notes found only in the C major scale. Below the staff are written the traditional names of each chord, along with their Roman numerals - capitalized or lower case depending on the quality (major or minor) of the first interval of a third. The capital Roman numerals indicate a major triad while the lower case Roman numerals indicate a minor triad. The common names for the chords in C major are also listed.

All of the other chords in tertiary harmony are constructed from the triads. The basic triads are extended by adding additional thirds, or altered by omitting specific chord tones. It is therefore essential for the reader to have a good working knowledge of basic triad construction and how these chords sound.

There are five, basic triads - major, minor, diminished, augmented, and the flat five chord. Only the major, minor, and diminished chords occur naturally in the major scale.

Major triads are constructed in accordance with the following formula:

The interval from E to G is a minor third (G is sharped in the key of E)

The interval from C to E is a major third

Major triads are constructed of a major third followed by a minor third intervalically. Minor triads are constructed as follows:

The interval from F to A is a major third

The interval from D to F is a minor third (F is sharped in the key of D)

Minor triads are constructed of a minor third followed by a major third. The diminished triads are constructed as follows:

The interval from D to F is a minor third

The interval from B to D is a minor third (D is sharped in the key of B)

Diminished triads are constructed of a minor third followed by a minor third.
The quality of the interval is always judged by the major scale key signature of the lowest note in the interval being examined. Also, the spelling or voicing of the chord being analyzed may not have all of its notes stacked in thirds. If this is the case, re-arrange the notes to obtain the closest stacking of thirds possible and analyze from that point. For example:

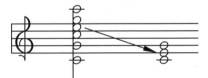

Since there are only C's, E's, and G's in this example, it is relatively easy to stack all of the constituent notes into thirds. Had the first chord contained additional pitches, however, the same process would have been used to analyze the chord. The chord name follows from the lowest note in the stack - in this case C major.

The augmented triad is constructed in accordance with the following formula:

The interval from E to G sharp is a major third

The interval from C to E is a major third

All augmented triads are constructed of a major third followed by another major third. The flat five triad is constructed as follows:

The interval from E to G flat is a diminished third

The interval from C to E is a major third

The interval from C to G flat is a diminished fifth

Note that all of the triads for any major scale, regardless of the key, are the same quality as the triads for the C major scale. In other words, all I chords are major, all ii chords are minor, all iii chords are minor, etc. This is true for all of the chord extensions and it is true for all scales of the same type, i.e. all Harmonic minor scales have the same chords. This is demonstrated in the harmonic matrices.

Seventh chords are another very important chord type used in every type of music. The seventh chords are created by stacking another third over the basic triad. The C major scale harmonized in seventh chords is as follows:

4

CHORD CONSTRUCTION - continued

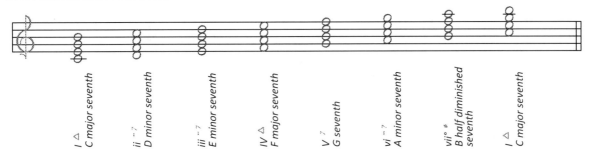

A major seventh chord is constructed by adding a major seventh interval to a major triad. It is an interval of a major third above the fifth in the chord. In the following example, a B note is added to the C major triad. B is a major seventh from C and a major third from G.

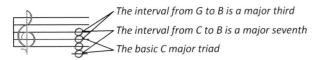

A minor seventh chord is constructed by adding a minor seventh interval to a minor triad. It is an interval of a minor third above the fifth in the chord. In the following example a C note is added to the D minor triad. C is a minor seventh from D and minor third from A.

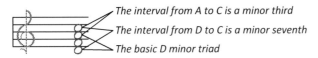

A dominant seventh chord, or simply seventh chord, is constructed by adding a minor seventh interval to a major triad. It occurs naturally over the dominant or V chord in a major scale. In the C major scale, it occurs over the G major chord.

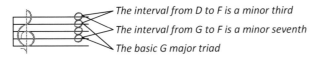

The last seventh chord to occur naturally in the major scale is the half diminished chord. It is formed by adding a minor seventh interval to the diminished chord. Notice that the interval between the fifth and seventh scale degrees is a major third. This is what distinguishes the half diminished chord from the full diminished chord, which is constructed of three minor thirds and has a minor third interval between the fifth and seventh degrees.

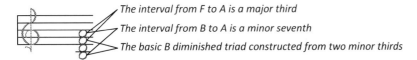

5

The remaining seventh chords are derived from altered scales. Note that any scale can be used to establish a system of diatonic harmony. The C major scale has been used in the examples merely as a convenience since it contains no sharps or flats, and because the basic naming conventions for intervals are derived from the major scale.

The diminished seventh chord is constructed by adding a diminished seventh interval to a diminished triad, resulting in three minor thirds.

The interval from G flat to B double flat is a minor third

The interval from C to B double flat is a diminished seventh

The basic C diminished triad

The dominant seventh flat five chord is constructed by adding a minor seventh interval to a flat five triad.

The interval from G flat to B flat is a major third

The interval from C to B flat is a minor seventh

The basic C flat five triad

The dominant seventh augmented, or simply seventh augmented chord, is constructed by adding a minor seventh interval to an augmented triad.

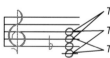

The interval from G sharp to B flat is a diminished third

The interval from C to B flat is a minor seventh

The basic C augmented triad

The minor major seventh chord is constructed by adding as major seventh to a minor triad.

The interval from G to B is a major third

The interval from C to B is a major seventh

The basic C minor triad

The major seventh flat five chord is constructed by adding a major seventh interval to a flat five chord.

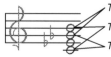

The interval from G flat to B is an augmented third

The interval from C to B is a major seventh

The basic C flat five triad

The major seventh diminished chord is constructed by adding a major seventh interval to a diminished chord.

The interval from G flat to B is an augmented third

The interval from C to B is a major seventh

The basic C diminished triad

The major seventh augmented chord is arrived at by adding a major seventh interval to an augmented triad.

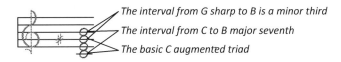

The interval from G sharp to B is a minor third

The interval from C to B major seventh

The basic C augmented triad

The minor major seventh/augmented fifth is constructed from a minor third, augmented fifth, and a major seventh.

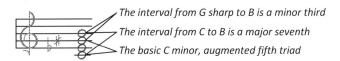

The interval from G sharp to B is a minor third

The interval from C to B is a major seventh

The basic C minor, augmented fifth triad

The ninth chords are formed by adding an additional third to the seventh chord, which is a ninth from the tonic. The eleventh chords and thirteenth chords follow in the same fashion - by stacking thirds. Naming conventions follow the same patterns as used with the triads and the seventh chords, with the basic triad being named followed by the descriptions of the upper extensions.

There are a few additional chord types that need to be discussed at this point. The first is the suspended second chords, or sus 2. The sus 2 chords are formed by replacing the third in the basic triad, dominant seventh and major seventh chord forms with a major second. Second, the suspended chords, or sus chords. These chords are formed by replacing the third in the basic triad, dominant seventh and major seventh chord forms with a perfect fourth. There are four forms of sixth chord that modify major and minor triads by adding either a minor or major sixth to the basic triad. Additionally, there is a seven/six chord that adds a major sixth to the dominant seventh chord and the nine/ six and minor nine/six chords which both have major sixths replacing sevenths in the major ninth and minor ninth chords.

All of the chord forms that "fall out" of a particular scale are spelled on a musical staff, indicated with a tablature type chord diagram, and shown in arpeggio form with their scale degrees numbered, which corresponds also to the formula of the chord as it relates to the major scale. The chord forms as described here also form the rows of the harmonic matrices used to describe the diatonic harmony of a key.

MODES

In the context of this text, modes are types of scales, constructed by using the pitches of a parent scale, but beginning and ending on different pitches of that parent scale. This rearranges the intervalic order of the parent scale. For example, in examining the intervallic relationships of a C major scale it is apparent that the intervals between adjacent pitches follow a pattern of 1, 1, 1/2, 1, 1, 1, 1/2 (1 designating a whole step and 1/2 designating one half step). The second mode would begin and end on the second pitch - or D in the case of the C major scale. This produces an intervallic pattern of 1, 1/2, 1, 1, 1, 1/2, 1. The third mode would begin and end on E and have the intervallic pattern of 1/2, 1, 1, 1, 1/2, 1, 1, etc.

I MODE - C IONIAN (C MAJOR)

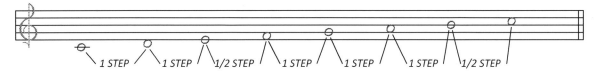

7

MODES - continued

ii MODE - D DORIAN

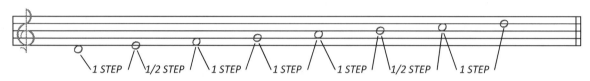

iii MODE - E PHRYGIAN

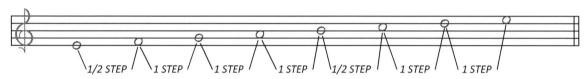

IV MODE - F LYDIAN

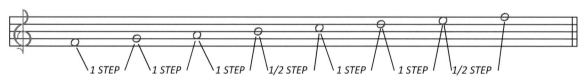

V MODE - G MIXOLYDIAN

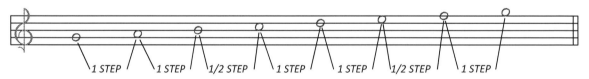

vi MODE - A AOLEAN (PURE MINOR)

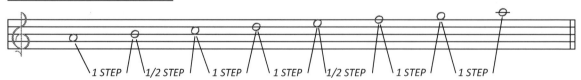

vii MODE - B LOCRIAN

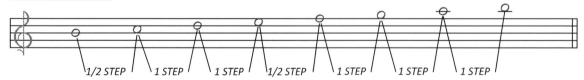

MODES - continued

As explained previously, the modes are numerically named with either a capitol or lower case Roman numeral, signifying the quality of the third interval (major or minor). The common names are included where they exist.

The sweeping patterns for the guitar lend themselves ideally to the study of the modes, in that each variation for a particular scale starts on a different pitch which corresponds directly to a mode pattern. For example, the second sweeping pattern in the key of F Major, while still being an F Major scale, is also the G Dorian mode, and the fingering pattern for that dorian mode is the same for all dorian modes, regardless of the key.

Other Instruments

While this text is primarily written for the guitar, the harmonic matrices included have an applicability for any instrument or any player interested in knowing, at a glance, the modes and chords generated by a scale. This information is invaluable in terms of understanding options for soloing and harmonic alternatives, as well as an aid for composers.

ORGANIZATION - How to use this book

Volume 1 of this text consists of seven, basic, seven tone mode or scale patterns with their corresponding modes as they progress up the neck of the guitar, organized into "chapters". Where a mode has a commonly used name it is given following its numerical value as a sweeping pattern. All of the basic scales are given with F as the tonic, or key center. Volume 2 contains seven additional seven tone modes. Between the two volumes, this text describes, harmonically, all of the seven tone scales currently in use.

I MODE - F IONIAN (F MAJOR)

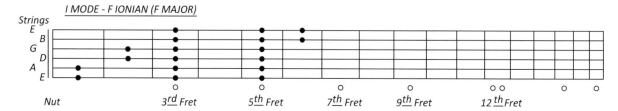

Immediately following the modes are the arpeggios of all of the chords generated by that scale, or the "diatonic" harmony generated by the mode. By definition, an arpeggio is "the notes of a chord played in succession". The notes listed are all of the notes that fall within the range of the given sweeping pattern. The arpeggios begin with the basic triad and follow a logical, numerical sequence, beginning with the simplest chords, progressing to the more complex chord extensions.

BASIC TRIAD - F MAJOR (1 3 5)

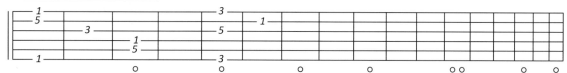

The arpeggios contain the numerical formula for each chord and show the scale degrees as they are located on the neck of the guitar.

Coupled with the arpeggios are the chords written on the staff with the formulas given as pitches rather than their numerical values. As in the arpeggios, followed by an example of the chord in diagram form. Note that the musical scores of the chord are the basic chord form and not always representative of the voicing of the chord diagram given.

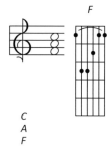

Again, keep in mind that the chord diagrams given as examples are an arbitrary choice. There are no specific reasons for the particular voicing shown. The chords should be added to a growing chord vocabulary which the player is continually expanding and experimenting with. It is said that there are over three thousand forms of the G7 chord between the nut and the twelfth fret. The particular voicing of a chord, as it is used in the context of a piece of music, is completely dependent upon the chord progression, the preceding and following chords, the melody, or solo, and the desired harmonic effect. Traditional rules of voice leading, doubling and spacing are subjects not addressed in this text.

Chord naming conventions and the symbols used are traditional and follow a widely accepted format. The basic chord name of a major chord is simply a capital letter, (F designates the F major chord). A minor chord is followed by a minus sign or dash. Diminished chords are followed by the "degree" sign, or °. Augmented chords are followed by a plus sign, or +. The suspended 2 chords are noted as sus 2, and the suspended 4 chords are simply noted as "sus". Major seventh, ninth chords, etc. are the numerical extension preceded by a triangle, (FΔ9 designates an F major ninth chord). Dominant chord forms are designated with the numerical value of the extension alone (F7 represents an F dominant seventh chord).

All mode patterns, arpeggio patterns, and chord forms are moveable. _EVERYTHING ON THE GUITAR IS MOVEABLE!_
This is one of the wonderful things about this particular instrument - or any stringed instrument for that matter. What this means to guitarists is that the F Ionian mode is fingered the same as a C Ionian mode - just starting from a different position on the neck.

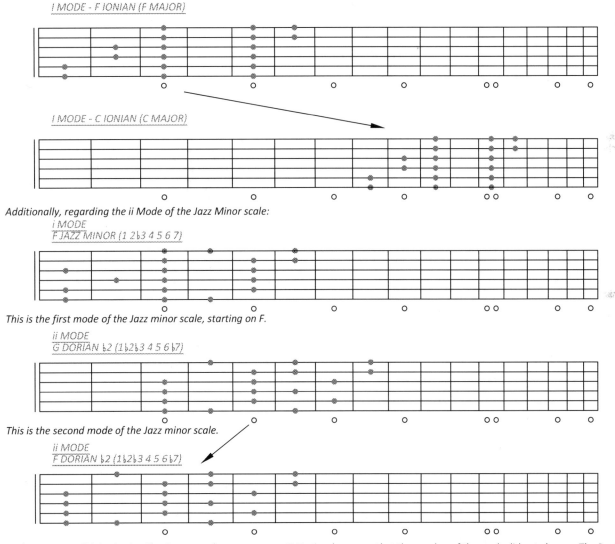

I MODE - F IONIAN (F MAJOR)

I MODE - C IONIAN (C MAJOR)

Additionally, regarding the ii Mode of the Jazz Minor scale:

i MODE
F JAZZ MINOR (1 2♭3 4 5 6 7)

This is the first mode of the Jazz minor scale, starting on F.

ii MODE
G DORIAN ♭2 (1♭2♭3 4 5 6♭7)

This is the second mode of the Jazz minor scale.

ii MODE
F DORIAN ♭2 (1♭2♭3 4 5 6♭7)

In this case, we slid the Dorian Flat 2 pattern down to start on F. Notice, however, that the number of the mode did not change. The Dorian Flat 2 mode is the second mode of the Jazz Minor scale regardless of the starting pitch. To find the diatonic harmony matrix is a simple matter of finding the matrix in which the F Dorian Flat 2 scale is the ii mode. In this case, the E Flat Jazz Minor scale and its harmonic matrix contains the diatonic chord forms that harmonize with this scale. Note that in some cases the "enharmonic equivalent" matrix may

11

have to be used. From the previous example one may have found the harmonic matrix to be D Sharp Jazz Minor, instead of E Flat Jazz Minor.

Another item to take note of is the upper and lower case Roman numeral numbering system of the modes. The Roman numerals are used so a distinction can be made regarding the quality of the third pitch in the mode. The quality of the third establishes the quality of the mode as major or minor. Capital Roman numerals indicate the scale contains a major third while lower case indicates a minor third.

The key note "F" is chosen as a starting place because of the convenience of moving the sweeping patterns up the neck in consecutive order, while minimizing the use of open strings. The matrices and patterns may be moved to any target location on the neck of the guitar. The order of the sweeping patterns, as they follow one another must however, remain constant. For example, selecting the key of "C" as our starting location for the I mode of the Major Scale:

I MODE - C IONIAN (C MAJOR)

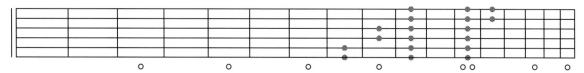

The next mode, which must follow is:

ii MODE - D DORIAN

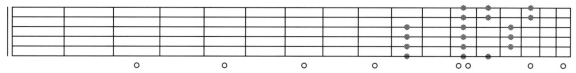

The next mode is the iii mode - E Phrygian. In this example a choice must be made whether to continue up the neck starting E-Phrygian on the twelfth fret, or at the nut using open strings. The nut and the twelfth fret are an octave apart and are synonymous for the purpose of moving the sweeping patterns.

iii MODE - E PHRYGIAN

OR:

iii MODE - E PHRYGIAN

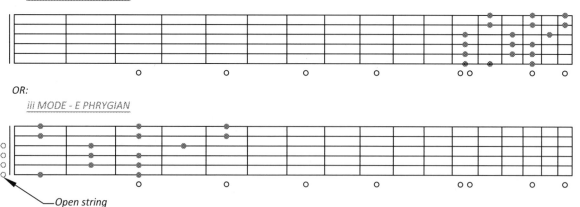

Open string

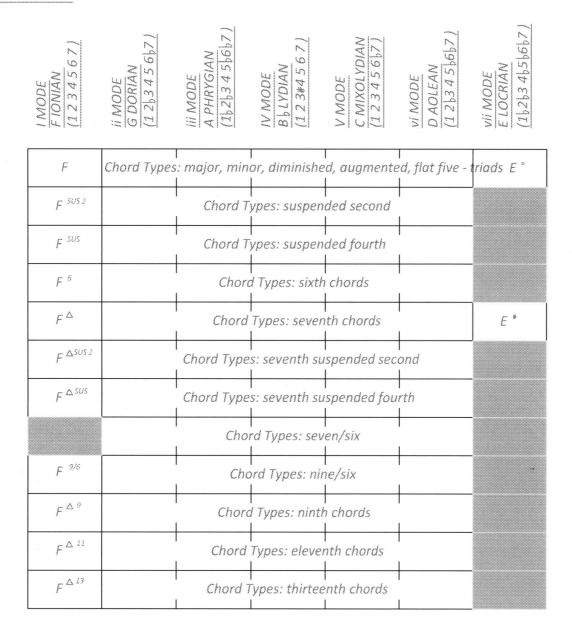

	I MODE F IONIAN (1 2 3 4 5 6 7)	ii MODE G DORIAN (1 2 ♭3 4 5 6 ♭7)	iii MODE A PHRYGIAN (1 ♭2 ♭3 4 5 ♭6 ♭7)	IV MODE B♭ LYDIAN (1 2 3 #4 5 6 7)	V MODE C MIXOLYDIAN (1 2 3 4 5 6 ♭7)	vi MODE D AOLEAN (1 2 ♭3 4 5 ♭6 ♭7)	vii MODE E LOCRIAN (1 ♭2 ♭3 4 ♭5 ♭6 ♭7)
F	Chord Types: major, minor, diminished, augmented, flat five - triads						E °
F SUS 2	Chord Types: suspended second						
F SUS	Chord Types: suspended fourth						
F 6	Chord Types: sixth chords						
F △	Chord Types: seventh chords						E ⁑
F △SUS 2	Chord Types: seventh suspended second						
F △SUS	Chord Types: seventh suspended fourth						
	Chord Types: seven/six						
F 9/6	Chord Types: nine/six						
F △ 9	Chord Types: ninth chords						
F △ 11	Chord Types: eleventh chords						
F △ 13	Chord Types: thirteenth chords						

The columns of each matrix in this book are labeled by; 1) A roman numeral, either capitalized or lower case, indicating a major or minor quality of the mode based upon the quality of the interval of the third degree in the scale. 2) The formal name of the mode, if one exists. 3) The numerical formula of the mode as it relates to the major scale.

The rows of each matrix are labeled with the types of chords indicated in the example above. If a specific chord type doesn't exist for a particular mode, the space for that chord is shaded grey.

EXAMPLE - of matrix application
This chord progression is taken from "Autumn Leaves" written by J. Kosma/J. Mercer/J. Prevert

There may be other matrices that would work over a set of changes or a given chord progression. The example shown is but one interpretation. A soloist may choose to change modes with each measure or each different chord. This example shows one of the many ways the harmonic matrices can be used for harmonic analysis.

THE MAJOR SCALE

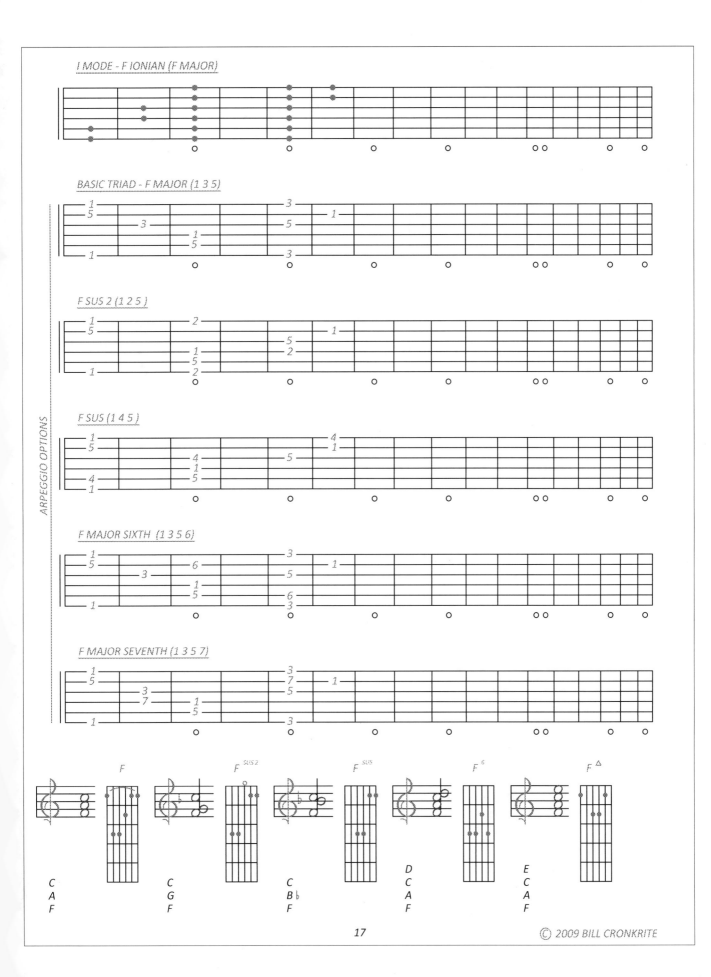

I MODE - F IONIAN (F MAJOR)

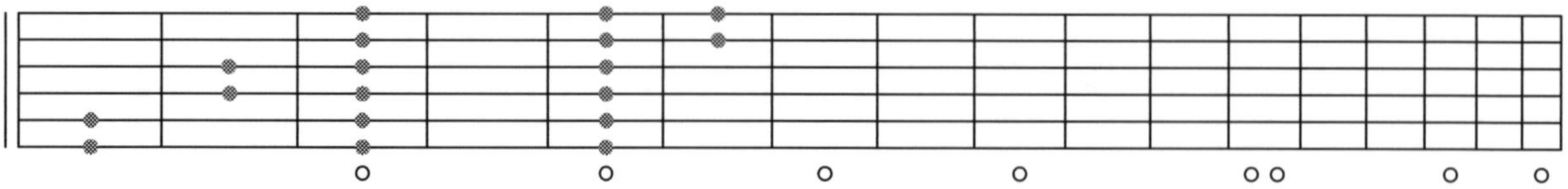

F MAJOR SEVENTH SUS 2 (1 2 5 7)

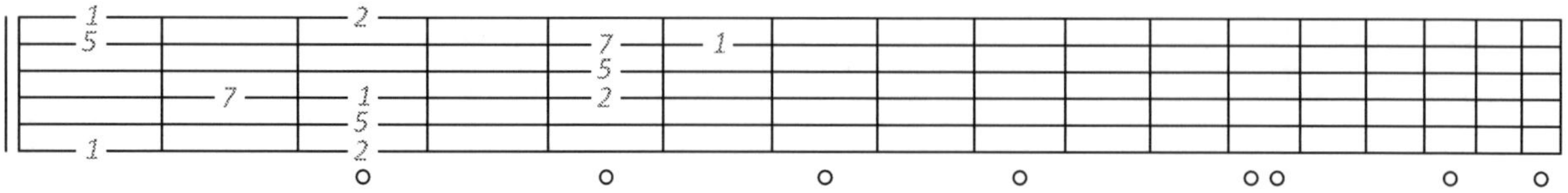

F MAJOR SEVENTH SUS (1 4 5 7)

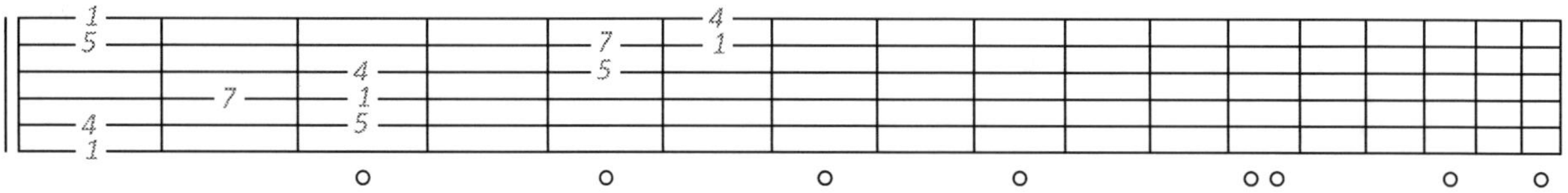

F MAJOR NINE/SIX (1 3 5 6 9)

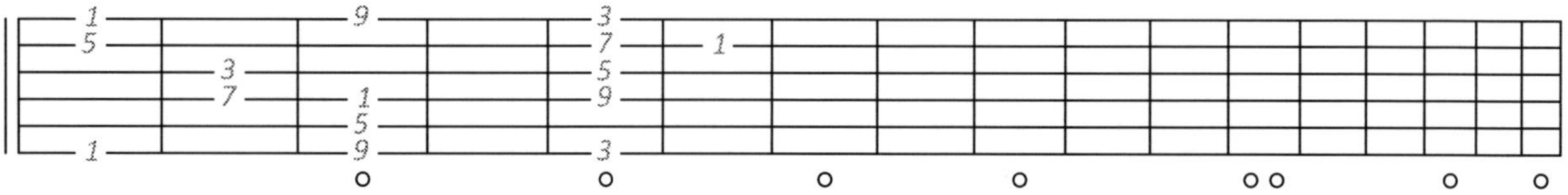

F MAJOR NINTH (1 3 5 7 9)

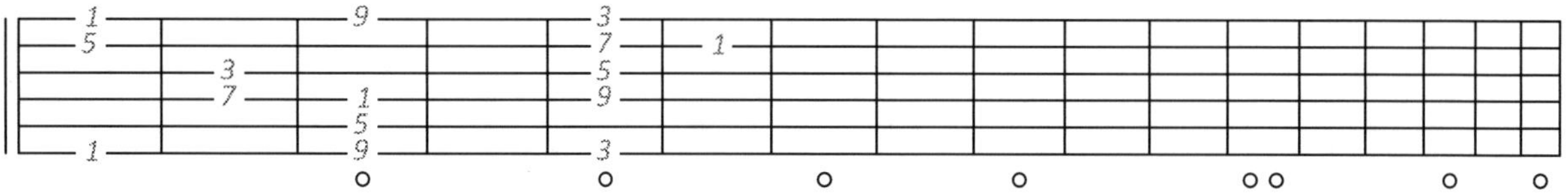

F MAJOR ELEVENTH (1 3 5 7 9 11)

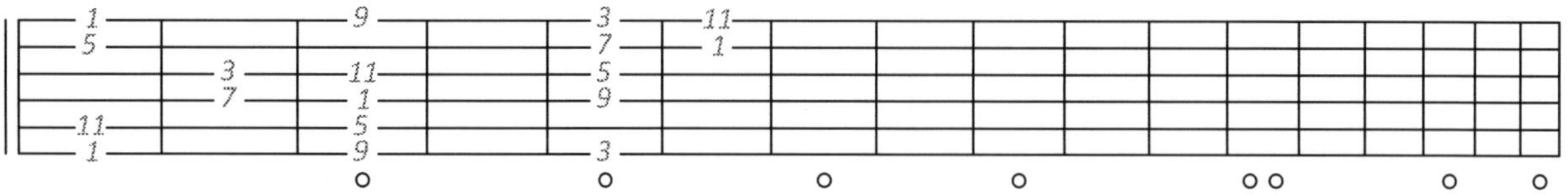

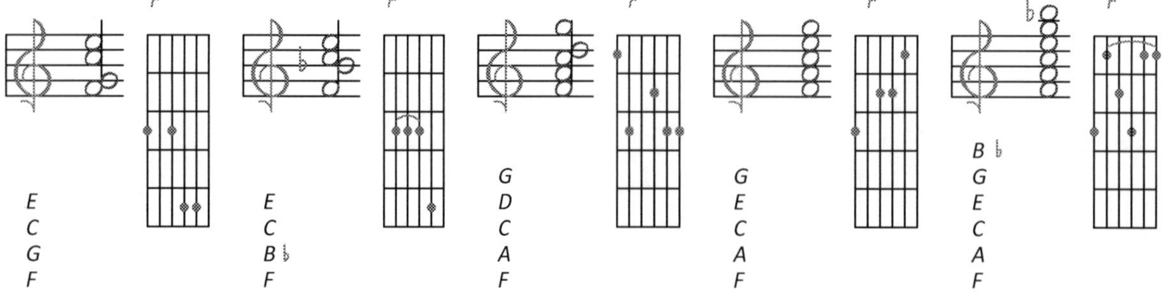

ARPEGGIO OPTIONS

$F^{\triangle SUS 2}$

$F^{\triangle SUS}$

$F^{9/6}$

$F^{\triangle 9}$

$F^{\triangle 11}$

E
C
G
F

E
C
B♭
F

G
D
C
A
F

G
E
C
A
F

B♭
G
E
C
A
F

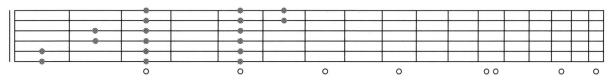

I MODE - F IONIAN (F MAJOR)

F MAJOR THIRTEENTH (1 3 5 7 9 11 13)

ARPEGGIO OPTIONS

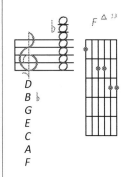

$F^{\triangle 13}$

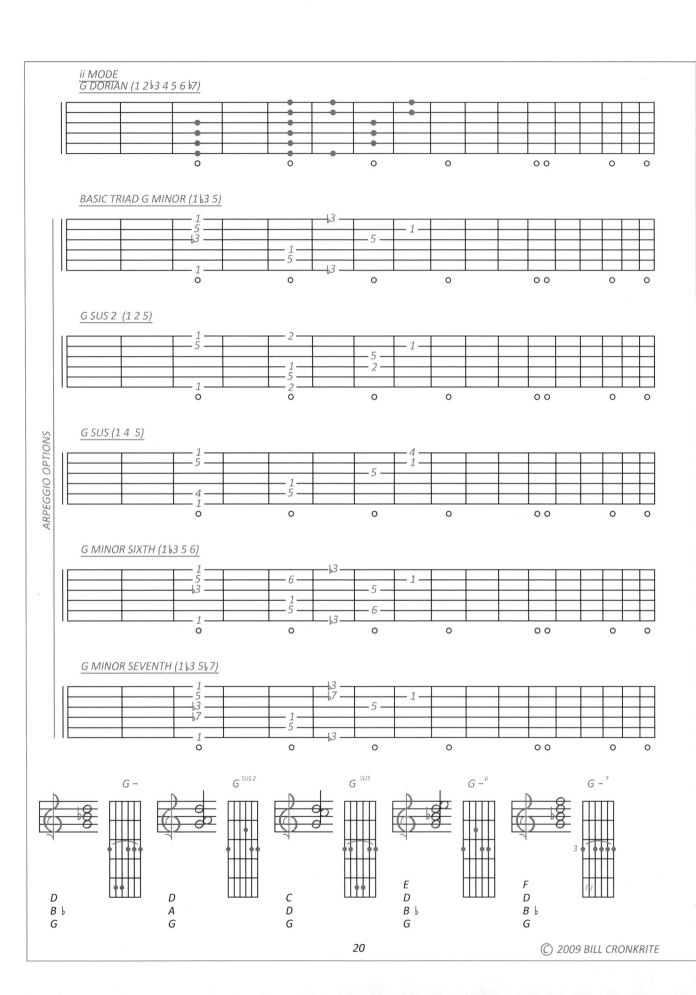

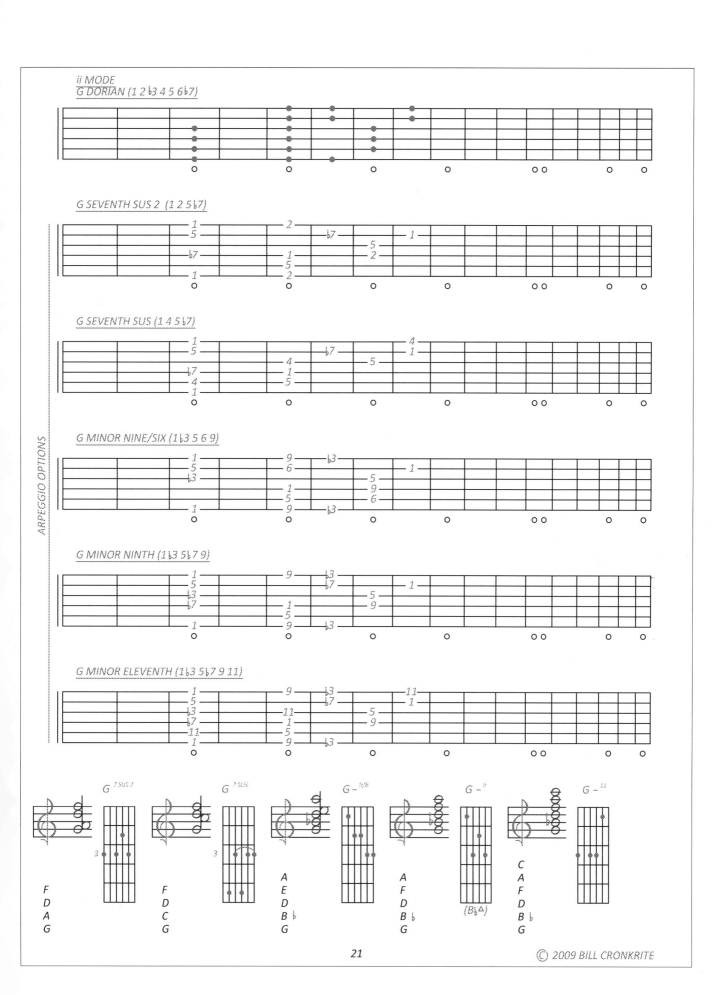

ii MODE
G DORIAN (1 2♭3 4 5 6♭7)

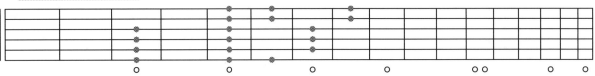

G MINOR THIRTEENTH (1 ♭3 5♭7 9 11 13)

ARPEGGIO OPTIONS

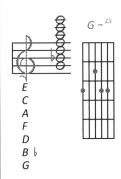

G –13

E
C
A
F
D
B ♭
G

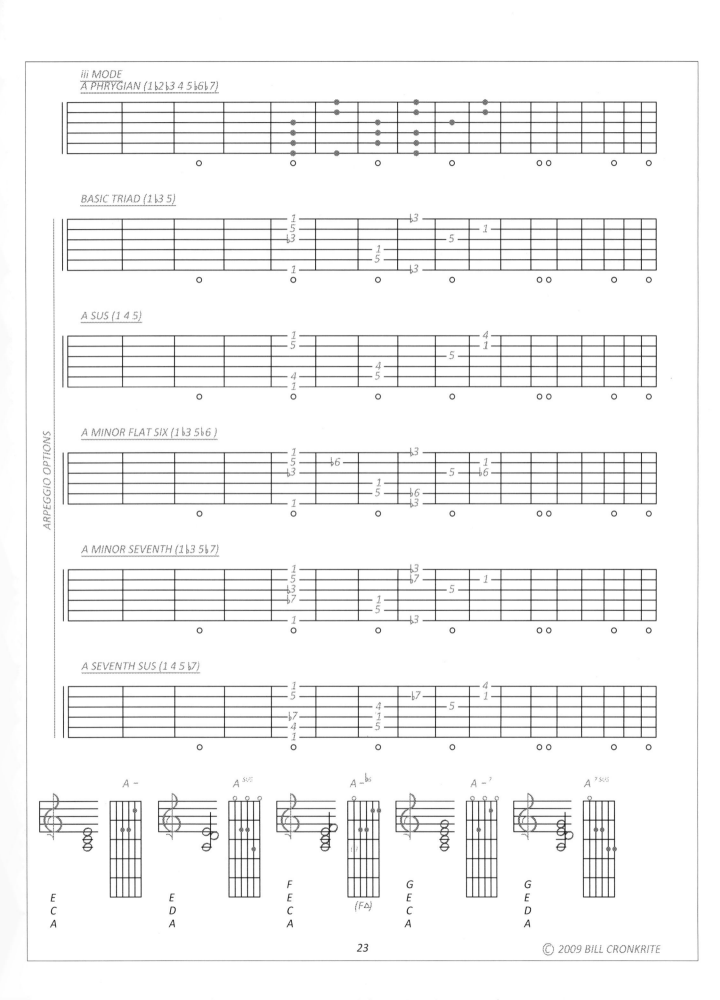

iii MODE
A PHRYGIAN (1 ♭2 ♭3 4 5 ♭6 ♭7)

BASIC TRIAD (1 ♭3 5)

A SUS (1 4 5)

A MINOR FLAT SIX (1 ♭3 5 ♭6)

A MINOR SEVENTH (1 ♭3 5 ♭7)

A SEVENTH SUS (1 4 5 ♭7)

ARPEGGIO OPTIONS

23

iii MODE
A PHRYGIAN (1♭2♭3 4 5♭6♭7)

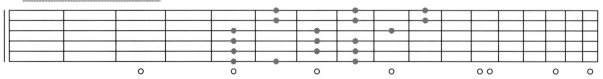

A MINOR SEVENTH FLAT NINE (1♭3 5♭7♭9)

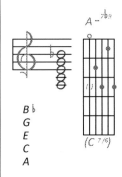

A -- $^{7\flat 9}$

$B\flat$
G
E
C
A

$(C^{7/6})$

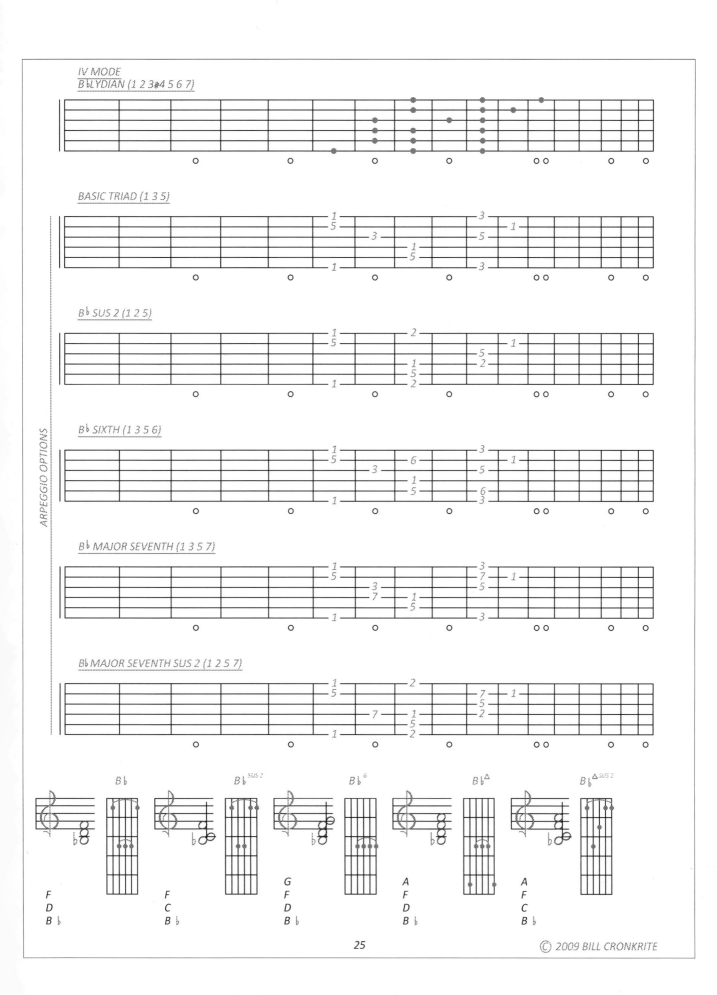

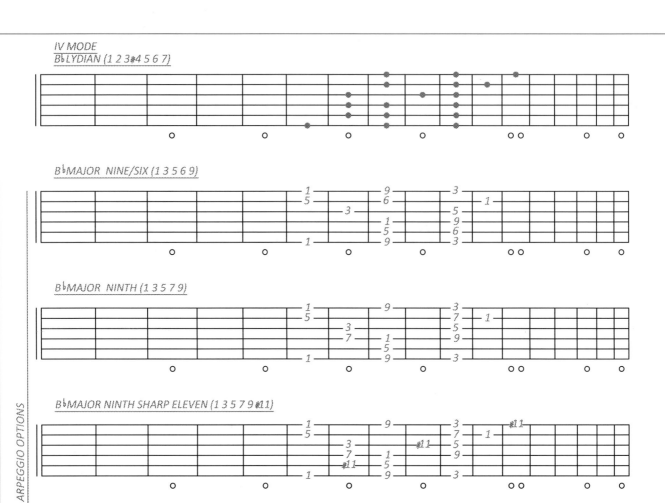

IV MODE
B♭ LYDIAN (1 2 3 ♯4 5 6 7)

B♭ MAJOR NINE/SIX (1 3 5 6 9)

B♭ MAJOR NINTH (1 3 5 7 9)

B♭ MAJOR NINTH SHARP ELEVEN (1 3 5 7 9 ♯11)

ARPEGGIO OPTIONS

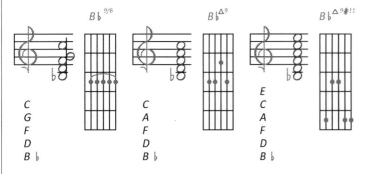

$B\flat^{9/6}$ $B\flat^{\Delta 9}$ $B\flat^{\Delta 9 \sharp 11}$

C
G
F
D
B♭

C
A
F
D
B♭

E
C
A
F
D
B♭

IV MODE
Bb LYDIAN (1 2 3#4 5 6 7)

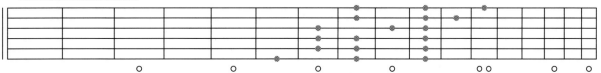

Bb MAJOR THIRTEENTH SHARP ELEVEN (1 3 5 7 9 #11 13)

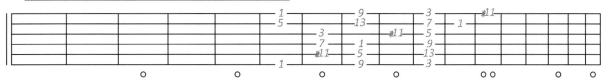

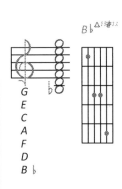

$B\flat^{\Delta 13 \#11}$

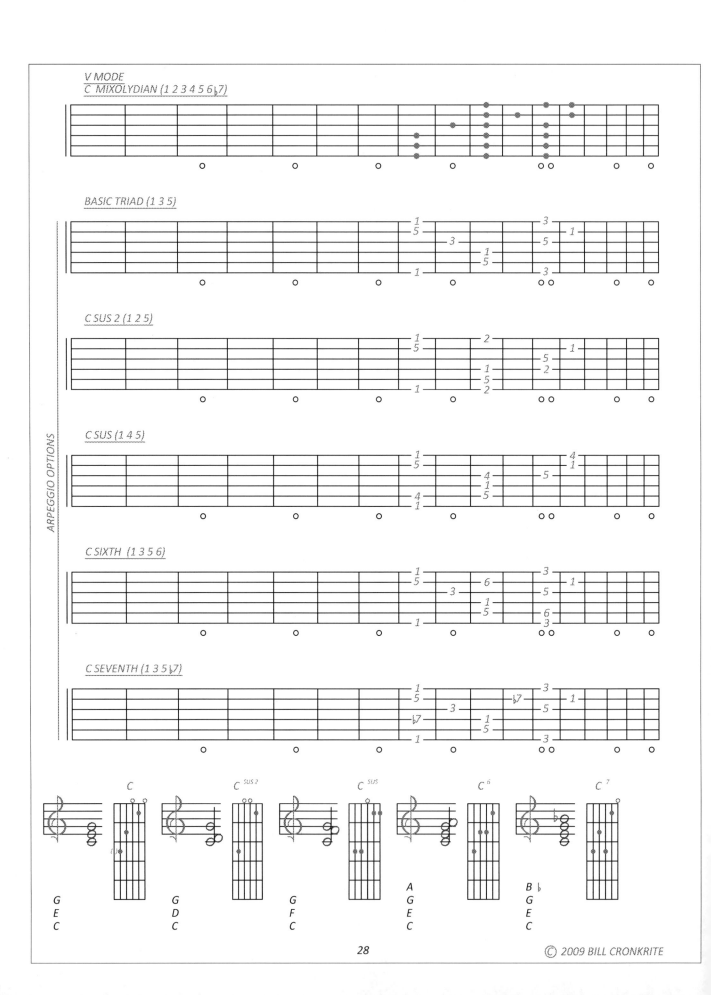

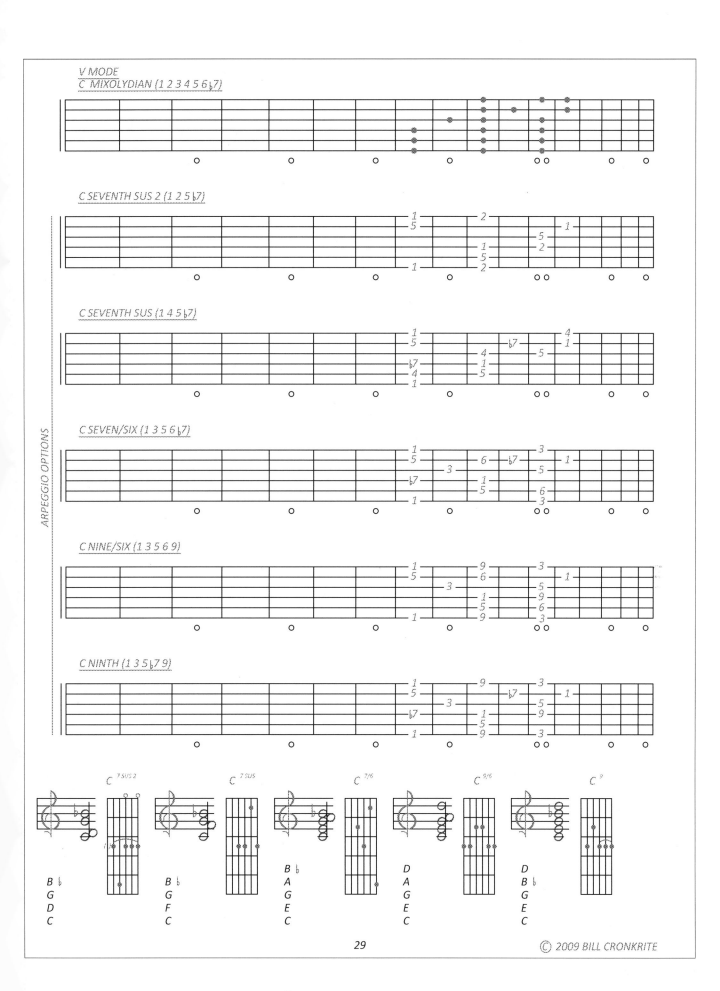

V MODE
C MIXOLYDIAN (1 2 3 4 5 6 ♭7)

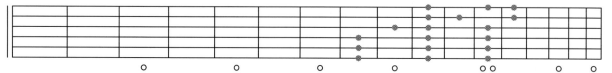

C ELEVENTH (1 3 5 ♭7 9 11)

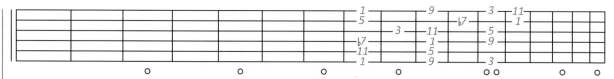

C THIRTEENTH (1 3 5 ♭7 9 11 13)

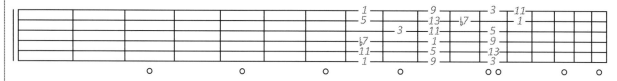

ARPEGGIO OPTIONS

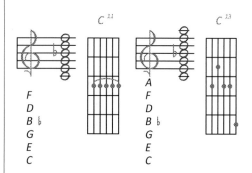

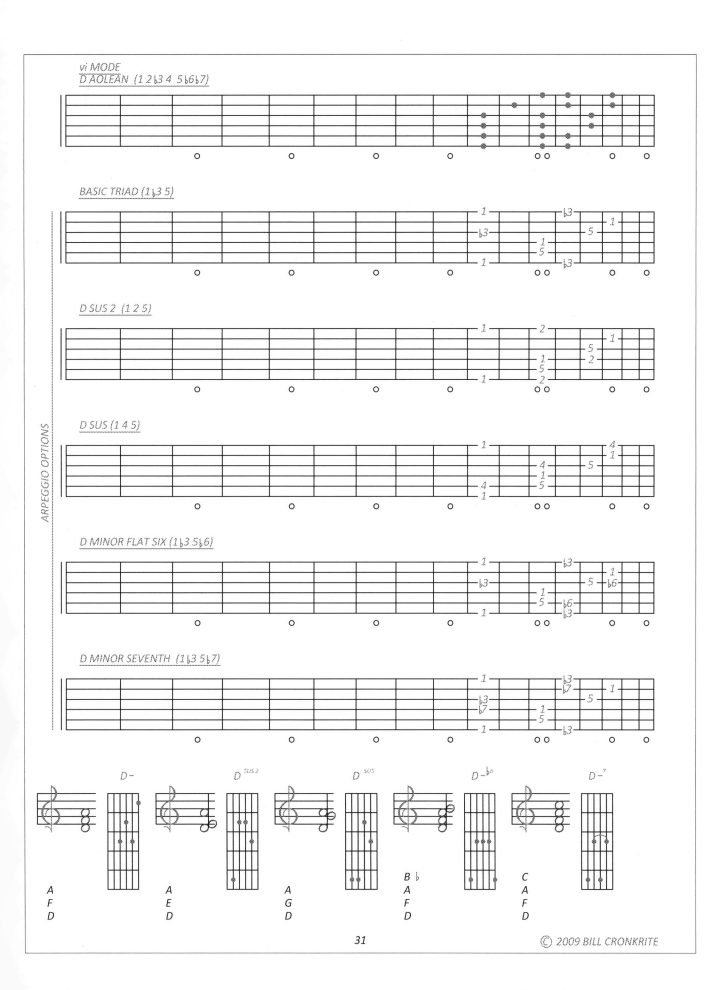

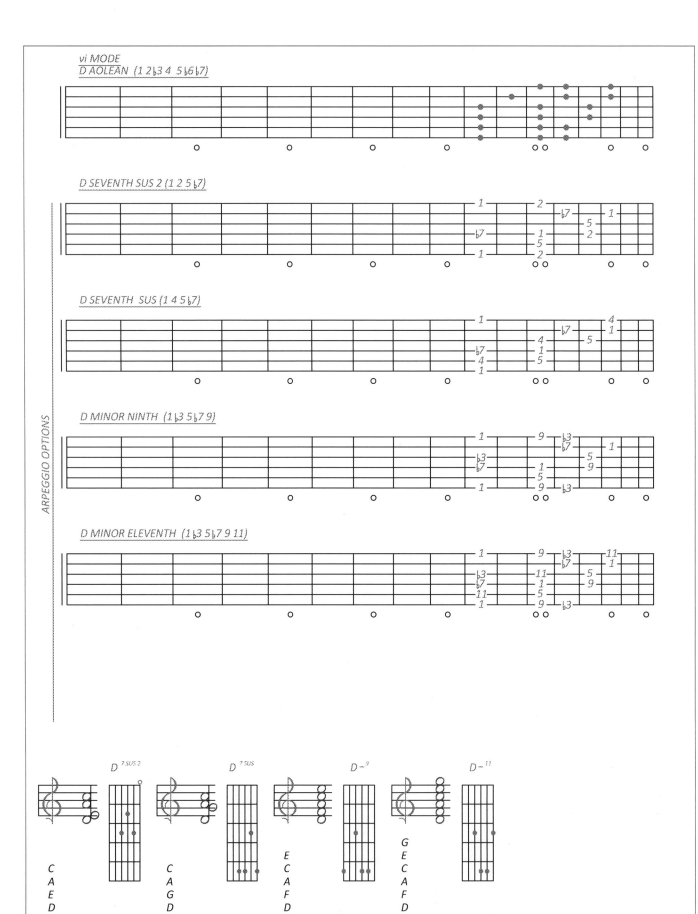

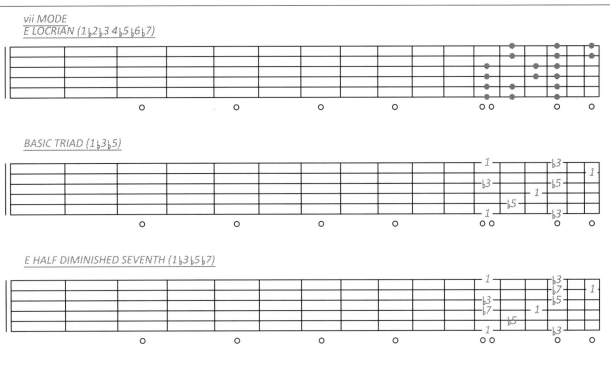

vii MODE
E LOCRIAN (1 ♭2 ♭3 4 ♭5 ♭6 ♭7)

BASIC TRIAD (1 ♭3 ♭5)

E HALF DIMINISHED SEVENTH (1 ♭3 ♭5 ♭7)

ARPEGGIO OPTIONS

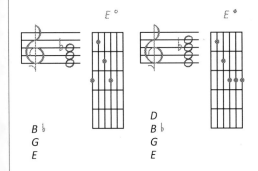

E °

E °

B ♭
G
E

D
B ♭
G
E

I MODE FIONIAN (1 2 3 4 5 6 7)	ii MODE G DORIAN (1 2b 3 4 5 6 b7)	iii MODE A PHRYGIAN (1 b2 b3 4 5 b6 b7)	IV MODE Bb LYDIAN (1 2 3 #4 5 6 7)	V MODE C MIXOLYDIAN (1 2 3 4 5 6 b7)	vi MODE D AOLEAN (1 2 b3 4 5 b6 b7)	vii MODE E LOCRIAN (1 b2 b3 4 b5 b6 b7)
F	$G{-}$	$A{-}$	$B\flat$	C	$D{-}$	$E°$
F^{sus2}	G^{sus2}		$B\flat^{sus2}$	C^{sus2}	D^{sus2}	
F^{sus}	G^{sus}	A^{sus}		C^{sus}	D^{sus}	
F^{6}	$G{-}^{6}$	$A{-}^{\flat6}$	$B\flat^{6}$	C^{6}	$D{-}^{\flat6}$	
$F^{\triangle}$	$G{-}^{7}$	$A{-}^{7}$	$B\flat^{\triangle}$	C^{7}	$D{-}^{7}$	$E^{\emptyset}$
$F^{\triangle sus2}$	G^{7sus2}		$B\flat^{\triangle sus2}$	C^{7sus2}	D^{7sus2}	
$F^{\triangle sus}$	G^{7sus}	A^{7sus}		C^{7sus}	D^{7sus}	
				$C^{7/6}$		
$F^{9/6}$	$G{-}^{9/6}$		$B\flat^{9/6}$	$C^{9/6}$		
$F^{\triangle 9}$	$G{-}^{9}$	$A{-}^{7\flat9}$	$B\flat^{\triangle 9}$	C^{9}	$D{-}^{9}$	
$F^{\triangle 11}$	$G{-}^{11}$		$B\flat^{\triangle 9\#11}$	C^{11}	$D{-}^{11}$	
$F^{\triangle 13}$	$G{-}^{13}$		$B\flat^{\triangle 13\#11}$	C^{13}		

I MODE F# IONIAN (1 2 3 4 5 6 7)	ii MODE G#DORIAN (1 2b 3 4 5 6 b7)	iii MODE A# PHRYGIAN (1 b2 b3 4 5 b6 b7)	IV MODE B LYDIAN (1 2 3 #4 5 6 7)	V MODE C#MIXOLYDIAN (1 2 3 4 5 6 b7)	vi MODE D#AOLEAN (1 2 b3 4 5 b6 b7)	vii MODE E#LOCRIAN (1 b2 b3 4 b5 b6 b7)
$F\#$	$G\#{-}$	$A\#{-}$	B	$C\#$	$D\#{-}$	$E\#^{\circ}$
$F\#^{sus2}$	$G\#^{sus2}$	▓	B^{sus2}	$C\#^{sus2}$	$D\#^{sus2}$	▓
$F\#^{sus}$	$G\#^{sus}$	$A\#^{sus}$	▓	$C\#^{sus}$	$D\#^{sus}$	▓
$F\#^{6}$	$G\#{-}^{6}$	$A\#{-}^{\flat 6}$	B^{6}	$C\#^{6}$	$D\#{-}^{\flat 6}$	▓
$F\#^{\triangle}$	$G\#{-}^{7}$	$A\#{-}^{7}$	$B^{\triangle}$	$C\#^{7}$	$D\#{-}^{7}$	$E\#^{\o}$
$F\#^{\triangle sus2}$	$G\#^{7sus2}$	▓	$B^{\triangle sus2}$	$C\#^{7sus2}$	$D\#^{7sus2}$	▓
$F\#^{\triangle sus}$	$G\#^{7sus}$	$A\#^{7sus}$	▓	$C\#^{7sus}$	$D\#^{7sus}$	▓
▓	▓	▓	▓	$C\#^{7/6}$	▓	▓
$F\#^{9/6}$	$G\#{-}^{9/6}$	▓	$B^{9/6}$	$C\#^{9/6}$	▓	▓
$F\#^{\triangle 9}$	$G\#{-}^{9}$	$A\#{-}^{7\flat 9}$	$B^{\triangle 9}$	$C\#^{9}$	$D\#{-}^{9}$	▓
$F\#^{\triangle 11}$	$G\#{-}^{11}$	▓	$B^{\triangle 9\#11}$	$C\#^{11}$	$D\#{-}^{11}$	▓
$F\#^{\triangle 13}$	$G\#{-}^{13}$	▓	$B^{\triangle 13\#11}$	$C\#^{13}$	▓	▓

I MODE G IONIAN (1 2 3 4 5 6 7)	ii MODE A DORIAN (1 2b3 4 5 6 b7)	iii MODE B PHRYGIAN (1 b2 b3 4 5 b6 b7)	IV MODE C LYDIAN (1 2 3 #4 5 6 7)	V MODE D MIXOLYDIAN (1 2 3 4 5 6 b7)	vi MODE E AOLEAN (1 2 b3 4 5 b6 b7)	vii MODE F# LOCRIAN (1 b2 b3 4 b5 b6 b7)
G	$A\text{-}$	$B\text{-}$	C	D	$E\text{-}$	$F\#^{\circ}$
$G^{SUS\,2}$	$A^{SUS\,2}$		$C^{SUS\,2}$	$D^{SUS\,2}$	$E^{SUS\,2}$	
G^{SUS}	A^{SUS}	B^{SUS}		D^{SUS}	E^{SUS}	
G^{6}	$A\text{-}^{6}$	$B\text{-}^{b6}$	C^{6}	D^{6}	$E\text{-}^{b6}$	
G^{Δ}	$A\text{-}^{7}$	$B\text{-}^{7}$	C^{Δ}	D^{7}	$E\text{-}^{7}$	$F\#$
$G^{\Delta SUS\,2}$	$A^{7\,SUS\,2}$		$C^{\Delta SUS\,2}$	$D^{7\,SUS\,2}$	$E^{7\,SUS\,2}$	
$G^{\Delta SUS}$	$A^{7\,SUS}$	$B^{7\,SUS}$		$D^{7\,SUS}$	$E^{7\,SUS}$	
				$D^{7/6}$		
$G^{9/6}$	$A\text{-}^{9/6}$		$C^{9/6}$	$D^{9/6}$		
$G^{\Delta 9}$	$A\text{-}^{9}$	$B\text{-}^{7\flat 9}$	$C^{\Delta 9}$	D^{9}	$E\text{-}^{9}$	
$G^{\Delta 11}$	$A\text{-}^{11}$		$C^{\Delta 9\#11}$	D^{11}	$E\text{-}^{11}$	
$G^{\Delta 13}$	$A\text{-}^{13}$		$C^{\Delta 13\#11}$	D^{13}		

I MODE Ab IONIAN (1 2 3 4 5 6 7)	ii MODE Bb DORIAN (1 2b 3 4 5 6 b7)	iii MODE C PHRYGIAN (1 b2 b3 4 5 b6 b7)	IV MODE Db LYDIAN (1 2 3 #4 5 6 7)	V MODE Eb MIXOLYDIAN (1 2 3 4 5 6 b7)	vi MODE F AOLEAN (1 2 b3 4 5 b6 b7)	vii MODE G LOCRIAN (1 b2 b3 4 b5 b6 b7)
Ab	$Bb-$	$C-$	Db	Eb	$F-$	$G°$
$Ab^{SUS\,2}$	$Bb^{SUS\,2}$		$Db^{SUS\,2}$	$Eb^{SUS\,2}$	$F^{SUS\,2}$	
Ab^{SUS}	Bb^{SUS}	C^{SUS}		Eb^{SUS}	F^{SUS}	
Ab^{6}	$Bb-^{6}$	$C-^{b6}$	Db^{6}	Eb^{6}	$F-^{b6}$	
$Ab^{\triangle}$	$Bb-^{7}$	$C-^{7}$	$Db^{\triangle}$	Eb^{7}	$F-^{7}$	$G^{ø}$
$Ab^{\triangle SUS\,2}$	$Bb^{7\,SUS\,2}$		$Db^{\triangle SUS\,2}$	$Eb^{7\,SUS\,2}$	$F^{7\,SUS\,2}$	
$Ab^{\triangle SUS}$	$Bb^{7\,SUS}$	$C^{7\,SUS}$		$Eb^{7\,SUS}$	$F^{7\,SUS}$	
				$Eb^{7/6}$		
$Ab^{9/6}$	$Bb-^{9/6}$		$Db^{9/6}$	$Eb^{9/6}$		
$Ab^{\triangle 9}$	$Bb-^{9}$	$C-^{7b9}$	$Db^{\triangle 9}$	Eb^{9}	$F-^{9}$	
$Ab^{\triangle 11}$	$Bb-^{11}$		$Db^{\triangle 9\#11}$	Eb^{11}	$F-^{11}$	
$Ab^{\triangle 13}$	$Bb-^{13}$		$Db^{\triangle 13\#11}$	Eb^{13}		

37

I MODE A IONIAN (1 2 3 4 5 6 7)	ii MODE B DORIAN (1 2♭3 4 5 6 ♭7)	iii MODE C# PHRYGIAN (1 ♭2 3 4 5 ♭6 ♭7)	IV MODE D LYDIAN (1 2 3 #4 5 6 7)	V MODE E MIXOLYDIAN (1 2 3 4 5 6 ♭7)	vi MODE F# AEOLIAN (1 2 ♭3 4 5 ♭6 ♭7)	vii MODE G# LOCRIAN (1 ♭2 3 4 ♭5 ♭6 ♭7)
A	B^{-}	$C\#^{-}$	D	E	$F\#^{-}$	$G\#^{\circ}$
A^{sus2}	B^{sus2}		D^{sus2}	E^{sus2}	$F\#^{sus2}$	
A^{sus}	B^{sus}	$C\#^{sus}$		E^{sus}	$F\#^{sus}$	
A^{6}	B^{-6}	$C\#^{-b6}$	D^{6}	E^{6}	$F\#^{-b6}$	
$A^{\triangle}$	B^{-7}	$C\#^{-7}$	$D^{\triangle}$	E^{7}	$F\#^{-7}$	$G\#^{ø}$
$A^{\triangle sus2}$	B^{7sus2}		$D^{\triangle sus2}$	E^{7sus2}	$F\#^{7sus2}$	
$A^{\triangle sus}$	B^{7sus}	$C\#^{7sus}$		E^{7sus}	$F\#^{7sus}$	
				$E^{7/6}$		
$A^{9/6}$	$B^{-9/6}$		$D^{9/6}$	$E^{9/6}$		
$A^{\triangle 9}$	B^{-9}	$C\#^{-7b9}$	$D^{\triangle 9}$	E^{9}	$F\#^{-9}$	
$A^{\triangle 11}$	B^{-11}		$D^{\triangle 9\#11}$	E^{11}	$F\#^{-11}$	
$A^{\triangle 13}$	B^{-13}		$D^{\triangle 13\#11}$	E^{13}		

I MODE Bb IONIAN (1 2 3 4 5 6 7)	ii MODE C DORIAN (1 2b 3 4 5 6 b7)	iii MODE D PHRYGIAN (1b 2b 3 4 5 b6 b7)	IV MODE Eb LYDIAN (1 2 3 #4 5 6 7)	V MODE F MIXOLYDIAN (1 2 3 4 5 6 b7)	vi MODE G AOLEAN (1 2b 3 4 5 b6 b7)	vii MODE A LOCRIAN (1b 2b 3 4 5 b6 b7)
Bb	$C-$	$D-$	Eb	F	$G-$	$A°$
Bb^{SUS2}	C^{SUS2}		Eb^{SUS2}	F^{SUS2}	G^{SUS2}	
Bb^{SUS}	C^{SUS}	D^{SUS}		F^{SUS}	G^{SUS}	
Bb^{6}	C^{-6}	D^{-b6}	Eb^{6}	F^{6}	G^{-b6}	
$Bb^{\triangle}$	C^{-7}	D^{-7}	$Eb^{\triangle}$	F^{7}	G^{-7}	$A^{\varnothing}$
$Bb^{\triangle SUS2}$	C^{7SUS2}		$Eb^{\triangle SUS2}$	F^{7SUS2}	G^{7SUS2}	
$Bb^{\triangle SUS}$	C^{7SUS}	D^{7SUS}		F^{7SUS}	G^{7SUS}	
				$F^{7/6}$		
$Bb^{9/6}$	$C^{-9/6}$		$Eb^{9/6}$	$F^{9/6}$		
$Bb^{\triangle 9}$	C^{-9}	D^{-7b9}	$Eb^{\triangle 9}$	F^{9}	G^{-9}	
$Bb^{\triangle 11}$	C^{-11}		$Eb^{\triangle 9\#11}$	F^{11}	G^{-11}	
$Bb^{\triangle 13}$	C^{-13}		$Eb^{\triangle 13\#11}$	F^{13}		

I MODE B IONIAN (1 2 3 4 5 6 7)	ii MODE C# DORIAN (1 2♭3 4 5 6 ♭7)	iii MODE D# PHRYGIAN (1 ♭2 ♭3 4 5 ♭6 ♭7)	IV MODE E LYDIAN (1 2 3 #4 5 6 7)	V MODE F# MIXOLYDIAN (1 2 3 4 5 6 ♭7)	vi MODE G# AOLEAN (1 2 ♭3 4 5 ♭6 ♭7)	vii MODE A# LOCRIAN (1 ♭2 ♭3 4 ♭5 ♭6 ♭7)
B	$C\#{-}$	$D\#{-}$	E	$F\#$	$G\#{-}$	$A\#^{\circ}$
B^{sus2}	$C\#^{sus2}$		E^{sus2}	$F\#^{sus2}$	$G\#^{sus2}$	
B^{sus}	$C\#^{sus}$	$D\#^{sus}$		$F\#^{sus}$	$G\#^{sus}$	
B^{6}	$C\#{-}^{6}$	$D\#{-}^{\flat 6}$	E^{6}	$F\#^{6}$	$G\#{-}^{\flat 6}$	
$B^{\triangle}$	$C\#{-}^{7}$	$D\#{-}^{7}$	$E^{\triangle}$	$F\#^{7}$	$G\#{-}^{7}$	$A\#^{ø}$
$B^{\triangle sus2}$	$C\#^{7 sus2}$		$E^{\triangle sus2}$	$F\#^{7 sus2}$	$G\#^{7 sus2}$	
$B^{\triangle sus}$	$C\#^{7 sus}$	$D\#^{7 sus}$		$F\#^{7 sus}$	$G\#^{7 sus}$	
				$F\#^{7/6}$		
$B^{9/6}$	$C\#{-}^{9/6}$		$E^{9/6}$	$F\#^{9/6}$		
$B^{\triangle 9}$	$C\#{-}^{9}$	$D\#{-}^{7\flat 9}$	$E^{\triangle 9}$	$F\#^{9}$	$G\#{-}^{9}$	
$B^{\triangle 11}$	$C\#{-}^{11}$		$E^{\triangle 9\#11}$	$F\#^{11}$	$G\#{-}^{11}$	
$B^{\triangle 13}$	$C\#{-}^{13}$		$E^{\triangle 13\#11}$	$F\#^{13}$		

I MODE C IONIAN (1 2 3 4 5 6 7)	ii MODE D DORIAN (1 2 b3 4 5 6 b7)	iii MODE E PHRYGIAN (1 b2 b3 4 5 b6 b7)	IV MODE F LYDIAN (1 2 3 #4 5 6 7)	V MODE G MIXOLYDIAN (1 2 3 4 5 6 b7)	vi MODE A AOLEAN (1 2 b3 4 5 b6 b7)	vii MODE B LOCRIAN (1 b2 b3 4 b5 b6 b7)
C	D-	E-	F	G	A-	B°
C$^{SUS\,2}$	D$^{SUS\,2}$		F$^{SUS\,2}$	G$^{SUS\,2}$	A$^{SUS\,2}$	
C^{SUS}	D^{SUS}	E^{SUS}		G^{SUS}	A^{SUS}	
C^{6}	D-^{6}	E-^{b6}	F^{6}	G^{6}	A-^{b6}	
C$^{\triangle}$	D-^{7}	E-^{7}	F$^{\triangle}$	G^{7}	A-^{7}	B$^{\o}$
C$^{\triangle SUS\,2}$	D$^{7\,SUS\,2}$		F$^{\triangle SUS\,2}$	G$^{7\,SUS\,2}$	A$^{7\,SUS\,2}$	
C$^{\triangle SUS}$	D$^{7\,SUS}$	E$^{7\,SUS}$		G$^{7\,SUS}$	A$^{7\,SUS}$	
				G$^{7/6}$		
C$^{9/6}$	D-$^{9/6}$		F$^{9/6}$	G$^{9/6}$		
C$^{\triangle 9}$	D-^{9}	E-^{7b9}	F$^{\triangle 9}$	G^{9}	A-^{9}	
C$^{\triangle 11}$	D-^{11}		F$^{\triangle 9\#11}$	G^{11}	A-^{11}	
C$^{\triangle 13}$	D-^{13}		F$^{\triangle 13\#11}$	G^{13}		

I MODE Db IONIAN (1 2 3 4 5 6 7)	ii MODE Eb DORIAN (1 2 b3 4 5 6 b7)	iii MODE F PHRYGIAN (1 b2 b3 4 5 b6 b7)	IV MODE Gb LYDIAN (1 2 3 #4 5 6 7)	V MODE Ab MIXOLYDIAN (1 2 3 4 5 6 b7)	vi MODE Bb AOLEAN (1 2 b3 4 5 b6 b7)	vii MODE C LOCRIAN (1 b2 b3 4 b5 b6 b7)
Db	Eb-	F-	Gb	Ab	Bb-	C°
Db$^{SUS\,2}$	Eb$^{SUS\,2}$		Gb$^{SUS\,2}$	Ab$^{SUS\,2}$	Bb$^{SUS\,2}$	
Db^{SUS}	Eb^{SUS}	F^{SUS}		Ab^{SUS}	Bb^{SUS}	
Db^{6}	Eb-^{6}	F-^{b6}	Gb^{6}	Ab^{6}	Bb-^{b6}	
Db$^{\Delta}$	Eb-^{7}	F-^{7}	Gb$^{\Delta}$	Ab^{7}	Bb-^{7}	C^{ø}
Db$^{\Delta SUS\,2}$	Eb$^{7\,SUS\,2}$		Gb$^{\Delta SUS\,2}$	Ab$^{7\,SUS\,2}$	Bb$^{7\,SUS\,2}$	
Db$^{\Delta SUS}$	Eb$^{7\,SUS}$	F$^{7\,SUS}$		Ab$^{7\,SUS}$	Bb$^{7\,SUS}$	
				Ab$^{7/6}$		
Db$^{9/6}$	Eb-$^{9/6}$		Gb$^{9/6}$	Ab$^{9/6}$		
Db$^{\Delta 9}$	Eb-^{9}	F-^{7b9}	Gb$^{\Delta 9}$	Ab^{9}	Bb-^{9}	
Db$^{\Delta 11}$	Eb-^{11}		Gb$^{\Delta 9\#11}$	Ab^{11}	Bb-^{11}	
Db$^{\Delta 13}$	Eb-^{13}		Gb$^{\Delta 13\#11}$	Ab^{13}		

I MODE D IONIAN (1 2 3 4 5 6 7)	ii MODE E DORIAN (1 2♭3 4 5 6 ♭7)	iii MODE F♯ PHRYGIAN (1 ♭2 ♭3 4 5 ♭6 ♭7)	IV MODE G LYDIAN (1 2 3 ♯4 5 6 7)	V MODE A MIXOLYDIAN (1 2 3 4 5 6 ♭7)	vi MODE B AOLEAN (1 2 ♭3 4 5 ♭6 ♭7)	vii MODE C♯ LOCRIAN (1 ♭2 ♭3 4 ♭5 ♭6 ♭7)
D	E -	F♯ -	G	A	B -	C♯°
D^{sus2}	E^{sus2}		G^{sus2}	A^{sus2}	B^{sus2}	
D^{sus}	E^{sus}	F♯^{sus}		A^{sus}	B^{sus}	
D^{6}	E-^{6}	F♯-$^{♭6}$	G^{6}	A^{6}	B-$^{♭6}$	
D$^{△}$	E-^{7}	F♯-^{7}	G$^{△}$	A^{7}	B-^{7}	C♯°
D$^{△sus2}$	E^{7sus2}		G$^{△sus2}$	A^{7sus2}	B^{7sus2}	
D$^{△sus}$	E^{7sus}	F♯^{7sus}		A^{7sus}	B^{7sus}	
				A$^{7/6}$		
D$^{9/6}$	E-$^{9/6}$		G$^{9/6}$	A$^{9/6}$		
D$^{△9}$	E-^{9}	F♯-$^{7♭9}$	G$^{△9}$	A^{9}	B-^{9}	
D$^{△11}$	E-^{11}		G$^{△9♯11}$	A^{11}	B-^{11}	
D$^{△13}$	E-^{13}		G$^{△13♯11}$	A^{13}		

I MODE Eb IONIAN (1 2 3 4 5 6 7)	ii MODE F DORIAN (1 2 b3 4 5 6 b7)	iii MODE G PHRYGIAN (1 b2 b3 4 5 b6 b7)	IV MODE Ab LYDIAN (1 2 3 #4 5 6 7)	V MODE Bb MIXOLYDIAN (1 2 3 4 5 6 b7)	vi MODE C AOLEAN (1 2 b3 4 5 b6 b7)	vii MODE D LOCRIAN (1 b2 b3 4 b5 b6 b7)
Eb	F -	G-	Ab	Bb	C -	D °
Eb $^{SUS\,2}$	F $^{SUS\,2}$		Ab $^{SUS\,2}$	Bb $^{SUS\,2}$	C $^{SUS\,2}$	
Eb ^{SUS}	F ^{SUS}	G ^{SUS}		Bb ^{SUS}	C ^{SUS}	
Eb ^{6}	F -^{6}	G -^{b6}	Ab ^{6}	Bb ^{6}	C -^{b6}	
Eb $^\triangle$	F -^{7}	G -^{7}	Ab $^\triangle$	Bb ^{7}	C -^{7}	D $^\emptyset$
Eb $^{\triangle SUS\,2}$	F $^{7\,SUS\,2}$		Ab $^{\triangle SUS\,2}$	Bb $^{7\,SUS\,2}$	C $^{7\,SUS\,2}$	
Eb $^{\triangle SUS}$	F $^{7\,SUS}$	G $^{7\,SUS}$		Bb $^{7\,SUS}$	C $^{7\,SUS}$	
				Bb $^{7/6}$		
Eb $^{9/6}$	F -$^{9/6}$		Ab $^{9/6}$	Bb $^{9/6}$		
Eb $^{\triangle 9}$	F -^{9}	G -^{7b9}	Ab $^{\triangle 9}$	Bb ^{9}	C -^{9}	
Eb $^{\triangle 11}$	F -^{11}		Ab $^{\triangle 9\#11}$	Bb ^{11}	C -^{11}	
Eb $^{\triangle 13}$	F -^{13}		Ab $^{\triangle 13\#11}$	Bb ^{13}		

I MODE E IONIAN (1 2 3 4 5 6 7)	ii MODE F# DORIAN (1 2b 3 4 5 6 b7)	iii MODE G#PHRYGIAN (1 b2 b3 4 5 b6 b7)	IV MODE A LYDIAN (1 2 3 #4 5 6 7)	V MODE B MIXOLYDIAN (1 2 3 4 5 6 b7)	vi MODE C#AOLEAN (1 2 b3 4 5 b6 b7)	vii MODE D# LOCRIAN (1 b2 b3 4 b5 b6 b7)
E	$F\#$	$G\#-$	A	B	$C\#-$	$D\#^{\circ}$
$E^{SUS\,2}$	$F\#^{SUS\,2}$		$A^{SUS\,2}$	$B^{SUS\,2}$	$C\#^{SUS\,2}$	
E^{SUS}	$F\#^{SUS}$	$G\#^{SUS}$		B^{SUS}	$C\#^{SUS}$	
E^{6}	$F\#-^{6}$	$G\#-^{b6}$	A^{6}	B^{6}	$C\#-^{b6}$	
$E^{\triangle}$	$F\#-^{7}$	$G\#-^{7}$	$A^{\triangle}$	B^{7}	$C\#-^{7}$	$D\#^{\emptyset}$
$E^{\triangle SUS\,2}$	$F\#^{7\,SUS\,2}$		$A^{\triangle SUS\,2}$	$B^{7\,SUS\,2}$	$C\#^{7\,SUS\,2}$	
$E^{\triangle SUS}$	$F\#^{7\,SUS}$	$G\#^{7\,SUS}$		$B^{7\,SUS}$	$C\#^{7\,SUS}$	
				$B^{7/6}$		
$E^{9/6}$	$F\#-^{9/6}$		$A^{9/6}$	$B^{9/6}$		
$E^{\triangle 9}$	$F\#-^{9}$	$G\#-^{7b9}$	$A^{\triangle 9}$	B^{9}	$C\#-^{9}$	
$E^{\triangle 11}$	$F\#-^{11}$		$A^{\triangle 9\#11}$	B^{11}	$C\#-^{11}$	
$E^{\triangle 13}$	$F\#-^{13}$		$A^{\triangle 13\#11}$	B^{13}		

THE JAZZ MINOR SCALE

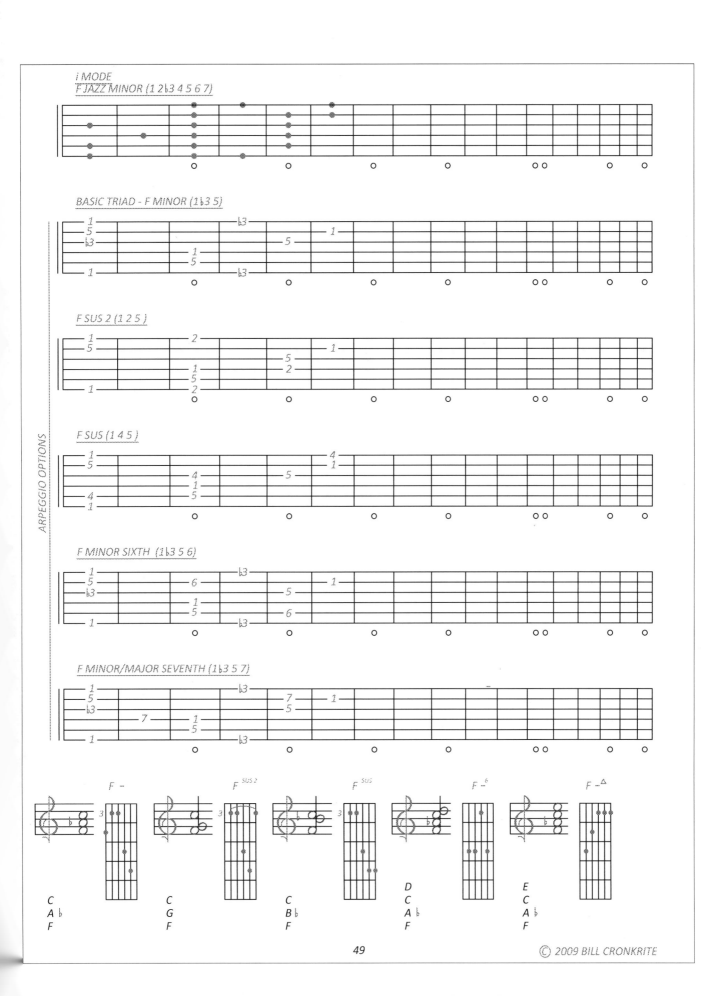

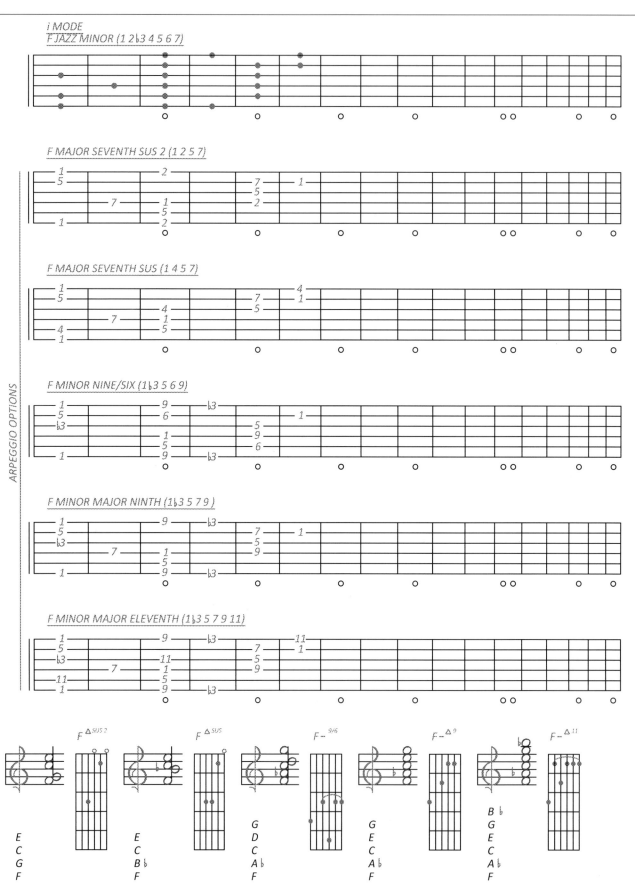

i MODE
F JAZZ MINOR (1 2 ♭3 4 5 6 7)

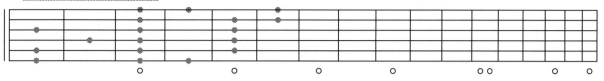

F MINOR/MAJOR THIRTEENTH (1 ♭3 5 7 9 11 13)

ARPEGGIO OPTIONS

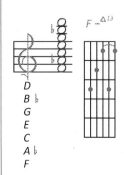

$F\,\text{-}^{\triangle 13}$

D
B ♭
G
E
C
A ♭
F

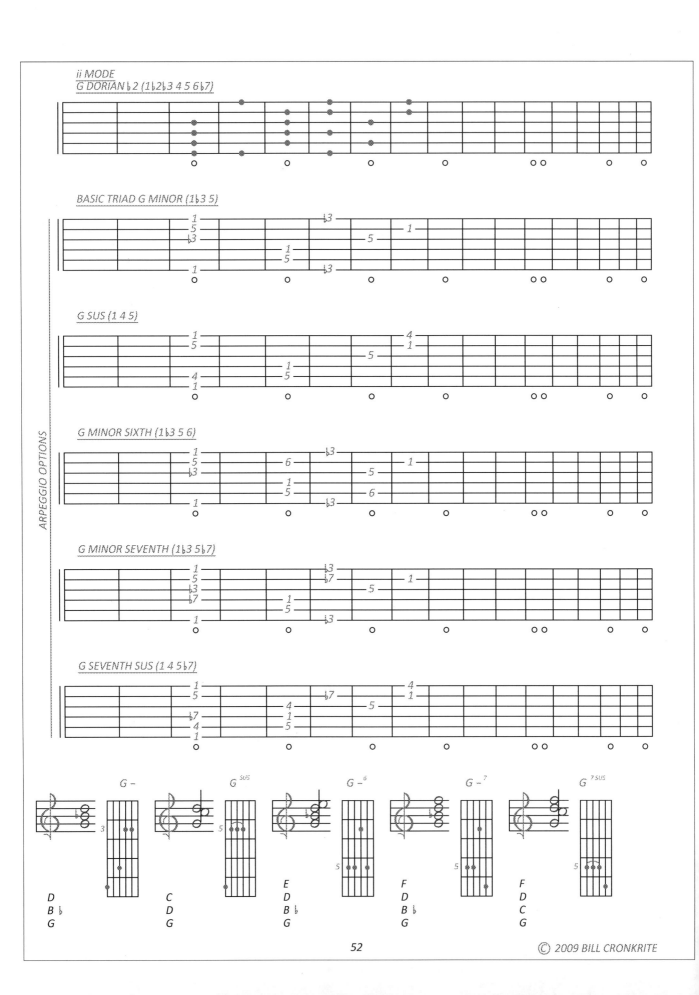

ii MODE
G DORIAN♭2 (1♭2♭3 4 5 6♭7)

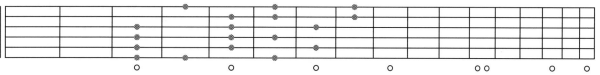

G MINOR NINE/SIX (1♭3 5 6 9)

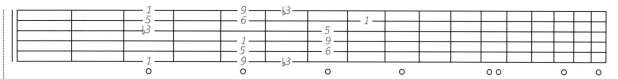

G MINOR FLAT NINE (1♭3 5♭7♭9)

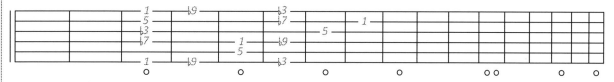

ARPEGGIO OPTIONS

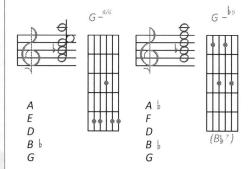

III MODE
A♭ LYDIAN AUGMENTED (1 2 3 ♯4 ♯5 6 7)

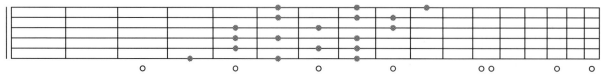

A♭ AUGMENTED (1 3 ♯5)

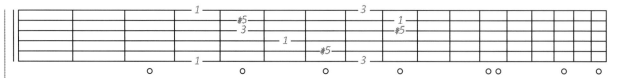

A♭ MAJOR SEVENTH SHARP FIVE (1 3 ♯5 7)

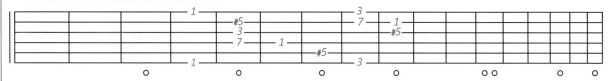

ARPEGGIO OPTIONS

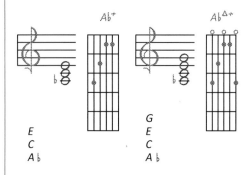

E
C
A♭

A♭⁺

G
E
C
A♭

A♭^{Δ+}

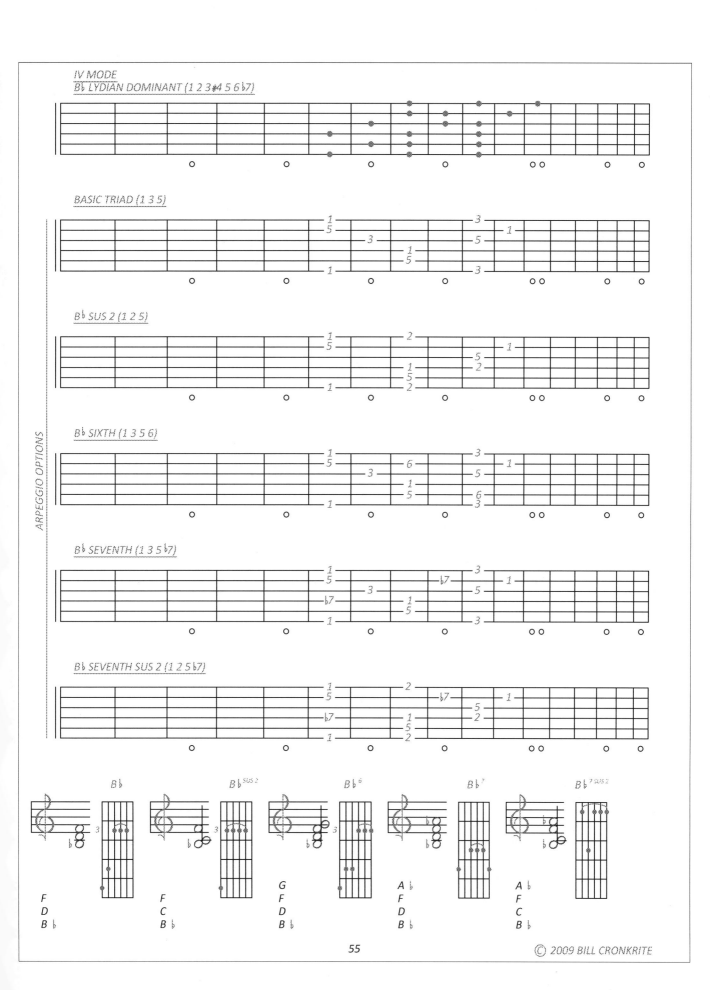

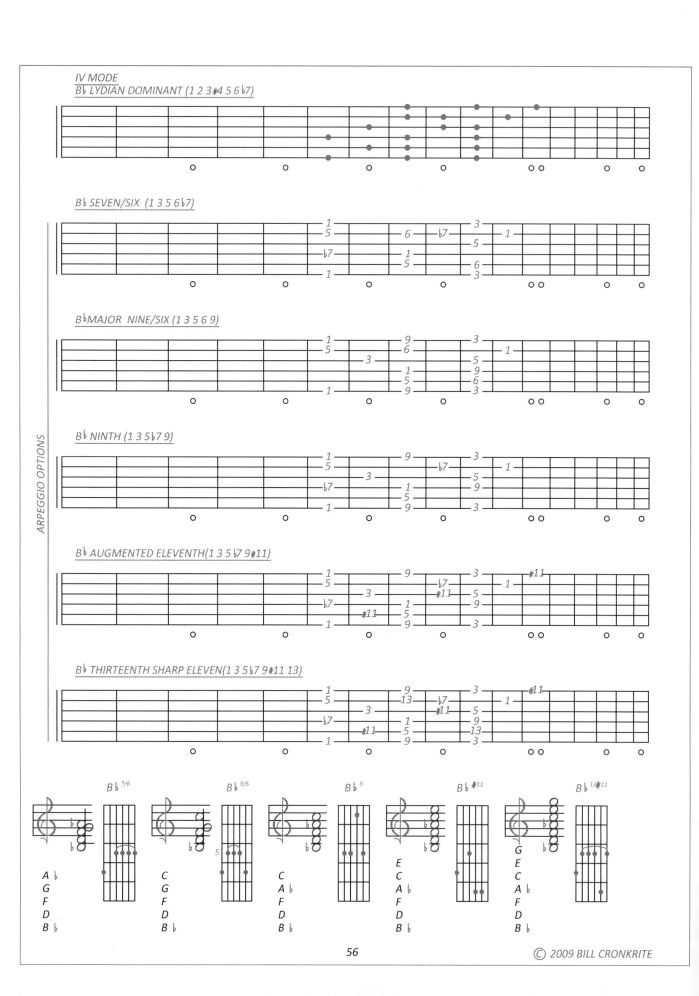

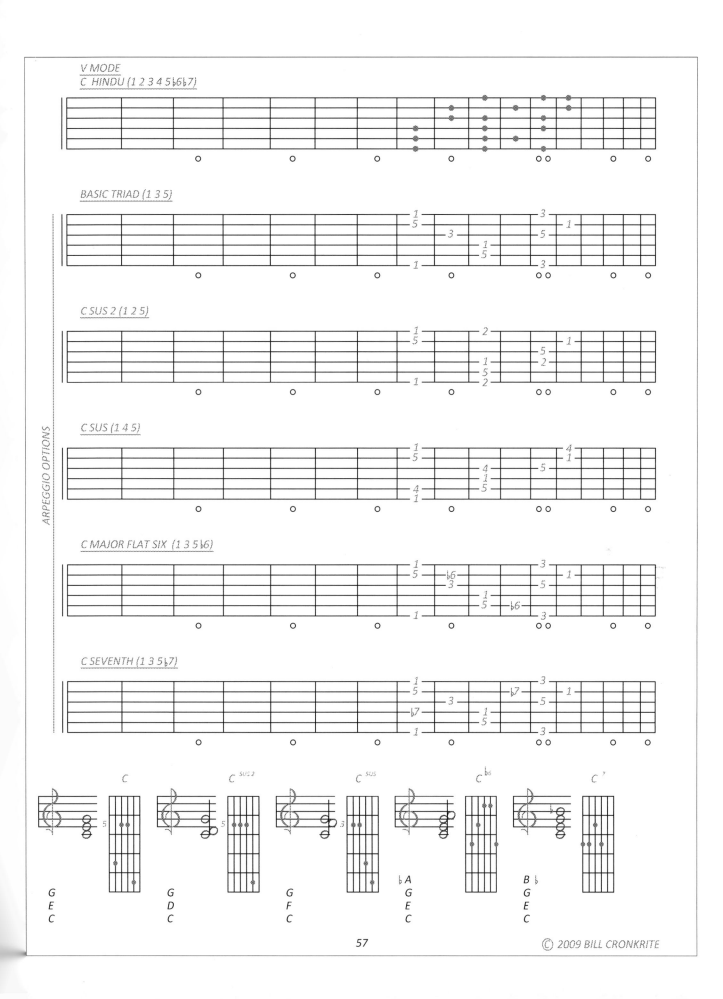

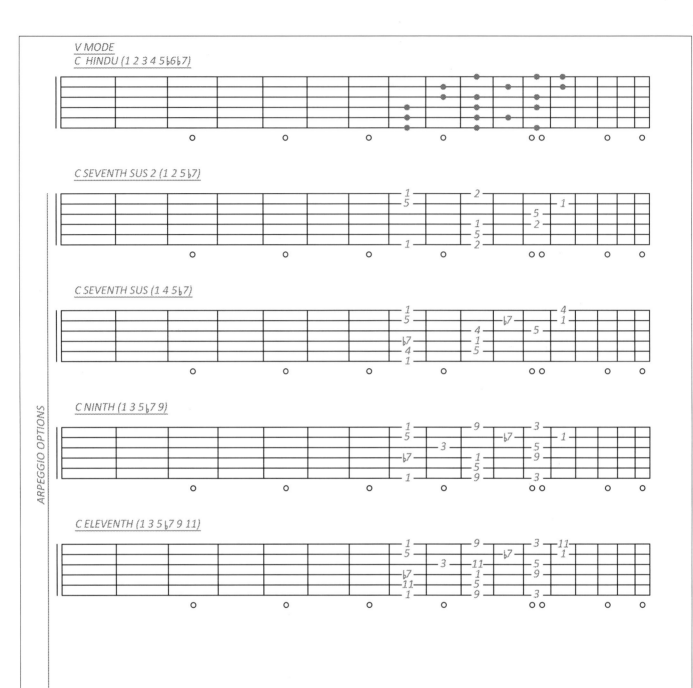

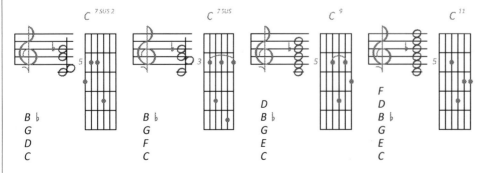

ARPEGGIO OPTIONS

vi MODE
D LOCRIAN ♭2 (1 2 ♭3 4 ♭5 ♭6 ♭7)

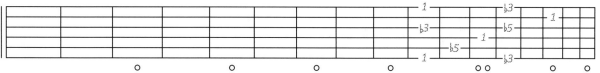

BASIC TRIAD (1 ♭3 ♭5)

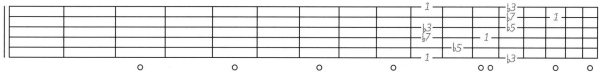

D HALF DIMINISHED SEVENTH (1 ♭3 ♭5 ♭7)

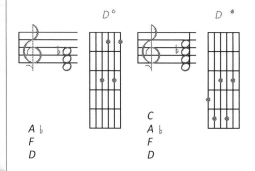

D°

D ∅

A ♭
F
D

C
A ♭
F
D

vii MODE
E SUPER LOCRIAN (1♭2♭3♭4♭5♭6♭7)

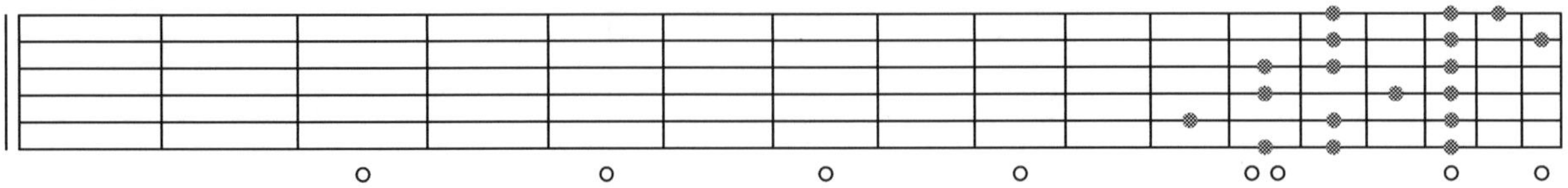

BASIC TRIAD (1♭3♭5)

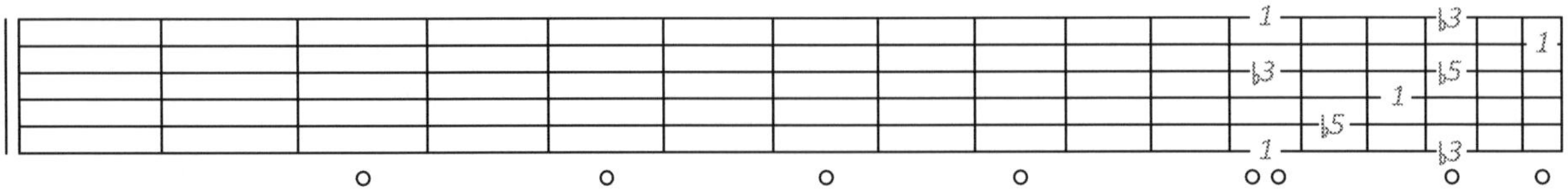

E HALF DIMINISHED SEVENTH (1♭3♭5♭7)

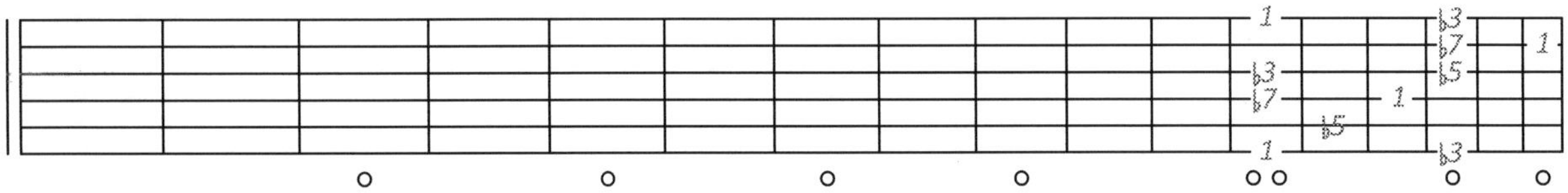

ARPEGGIO OPTIONS

E°

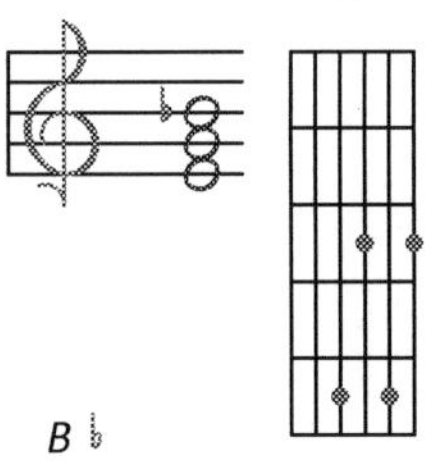

E°

B♭
G
E

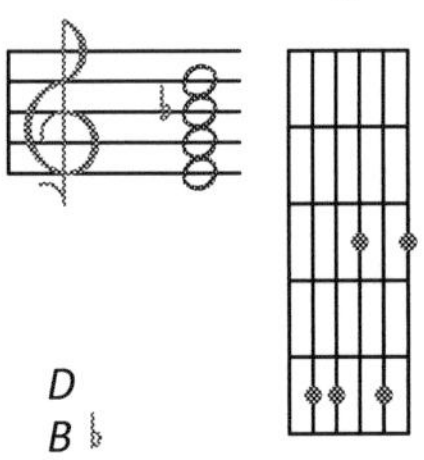

D
B♭
G
E

i MODE F JAZZ MINOR $(1\ 2\ \flat3\ 4\ 5\ 6\ 7)$	ii MODE G DORIAN $\flat2$ $(1\ \flat2\ \flat3\ 4\ 5\ 6\ \flat7)$	iii MODE $A\flat$ LYDIAN AUG. $(1\ 2\ 3\ \sharp4\ \sharp5\ 6\ 7)$	IV MODE $B\flat$ LYDIAN DOM. $(1\ 2\ 3\ \sharp4\ 5\ 6\ \flat7)$	V MODE C HINDU $(1\ 2\ 3\ 4\ 5\ \flat6\ \flat7)$	vi MODE D LOCRIAN $\natural2$ $(1\ 2\ \flat3\ 4\ \flat5\ \flat6\ \flat7)$	vii MODE E° SUPER LOCRIAN $(1\ \flat2\ \flat3\ \flat4\ \flat5\ \flat6\ \flat7)$
$F-$	$G-$	$A\flat^+$	$B\flat$	C	D°	E°
$F^{SUS\,2}$			$B\flat^{SUS\,2}$	$C^{SUS\,2}$		
F^{SUS}	G^{SUS}			C^{SUS}		
$F-^{6}$	$G-^{6}$		$B\flat^{6}$	$C^{\flat6}$		
$F-^{\triangle}$	$G-^{7}$	$A\flat^{\triangle+}$	$B\flat^{7}$	C^{7}	D^*	E^*
$F^{\triangle SUS\,2}$			$B\flat^{7\,SUS\,2}$	$C^{7\,SUS\,2}$		
$F^{\triangle SUS}$	$G^{7\,SUS}$			$C^{7\,SUS}$		
			$B\flat^{7/6}$			
$F-^{9/6}$	$G-^{9/6}$		$B\flat^{9/6}$			
$F-^{\triangle 9}$	$G-^{\flat9}$		$B\flat^{9}$	C^{9}		
$F-^{\triangle 11}$			$B\flat^{\sharp11}$	C^{11}		
$F-^{\triangle 13}$			$B\flat^{13\sharp11}$			

i MODE F# JAZZ MINOR (1 2 b3 4 5 6 7)	ii MODE G# DORIAN b2 (1 b2 b3 4 5 6 b7)	III MODE A LYDIAN AUG. (1 2 3 #4 #5 6 7)	IV MODE B LYDIAN DOM. (1 2 3 #4 5 6 b7)	V MODE C# HINDU (1 2 3 4 5 b6 b7)	vi MODE D# LOCRIAN ♮2 (1 2 b3 4 b5 b6 b7)	vii MODE E# SUPER LOCRIAN (1 b2 b3 b4 b5 b6 b7)
$F\#^{-}$	$G\#^{-}$	A^{+}	B	$C\#$	$D\#^{\circ}$	$E\#^{\circ}$
$F\#^{SUS\,2}$			$B^{SUS\,2}$	$C\#^{SUS\,2}$		
$F\#^{SUS}$	$G\#^{SUS}$			$C\#^{SUS}$		
$F\#^{-6}$	$G\#^{-6}$		B^{6}	$C\#^{b6}$		
$F\#^{-\Delta}$	$G\#^{-7}$	$A^{\Delta+}$	B^{7}	$C\#^{7}$	$D\#^{\varnothing}$	$E\#^{\varnothing}$
$F\#^{\Delta SUS\,2}$			$B^{7\,SUS\,2}$	$C\#^{7\,SUS\,2}$		
$F\#^{\Delta SUS}$	$G\#^{7\,SUS}$			$C\#^{7\,SUS}$		
			$B^{7/6}$			
$F\#^{-9/6}$	$G\#^{-9/6}$		$B^{9/6}$			
$F\#^{-\Delta 9}$	$G\#^{-b9}$		B^{9}	$C\#^{9}$		
$F\#^{-\Delta 11}$			$B^{\#11}$	$C\#^{11}$		
$F\#^{-\Delta 13}$			$B^{13\#11}$			

THE MATRIX

i MODE G JAZZ MINOR (1 2 b3 4 5 6 7)	ii MODE A DORIAN b2 (1 b2 b3 4 5 6 b7)	III MODE Bb LYDIAN AUG. (1 2 3 #4 #5 6 7)	IV MODE C LYDIAN DOM. (1 2 3 #4 5 6 b7)	V MODE D HINDU (1 2 3 4 5 b6 b7)	vi MODE E LOCRIAN ♮2 (1 2 b3 4 b5 b6 b7)	vii MODE F# SUPER LOCRIAN (1 b2 b3 b4 b5 b6 b7)
G^{-}	A^{-}	Bb^{+}	C	D	E°	$F\#^{\circ}$
$G^{SUS\,2}$			$C^{SUS\,2}$	$D^{SUS\,2}$		
G^{SUS}	A^{SUS}			D^{SUS}		
G^{-6}	A^{-6}		C^{6}	D^{b6}		
$G^{-\triangle}$	A^{-7}	$Bb^{\triangle+}$	C^{7}	D^{7}	$E^{\varnothing}$	$F\#^{\varnothing}$
$G^{\triangle SUS\,2}$			$C^{7\,SUS\,2}$	$D^{7\,SUS\,2}$		
$G^{\triangle SUS}$	$A^{7\,SUS}$			$D^{7\,SUS}$		
			$C^{7/6}$			
$G^{-9/6}$	$A^{-9/6}$		$C^{9/6}$			
$G^{-\triangle 9}$	A^{-b9}		C^{9}	D^{9}		
$G^{-\triangle 11}$			$C^{\#11}$	D^{11}		
$G^{-\triangle 13}$			$C^{13\#11}$			

63

i MODE Ab JAZZ MINOR (1 2 b3 4 5 6 7)	ii MODE Bb DORIAN b2 (1 b2 3 4 5 6 b7)	III MODE Cb LYDIAN AUG. (1 2 3 #4 #5 6 7)	IV MODE Db LYDIAN DOM. (1 2 3 #4 5 6 b7)	V MODE Eb HINDU (1 2 3 4 5 b6 b7)	vi MODE F LOCRIAN ♮2 (1 2 b3 4 b5 b6 b7)	vii MODE G SUPER LOCRIAN (1 b2 b3 b4 b5 b6 b7)
Ab-	Bb-	Cb+	Db	Eb	F°	G°
Ab^{sus2}			Db^{sus2}	Eb^{sus2}		
Ab^{sus}	Bb^{sus}			Eb^{sus}		
Ab-^{6}	Bb--^{6}		Db^{6}	Eb^{b6}		
Ab-$^{△}$	Bb-^{7}	Cb$^{△+}$	Db^{7}	Eb^{7}	F^{ø}	G^{ø}
Ab$^{△sus2}$			Db^{7sus2}	Eb^{7sus2}		
Ab$^{△sus}$	Bb^{7sus}			Eb^{7sus}		
			Db$^{7/6}$			
Ab-$^{9/6}$	Bb-$^{9/6}$		Db$^{9/6}$			
Ab-$^{△9}$	Bb-^{b9}		D^{b9}	Eb^{9}		
Ab-$^{△11}$			Db$^{#11}$	Eb^{11}		
Ab-$^{△13}$			Db$^{13#11}$			

THE MATRIX

i MODE A JAZZ MINOR (1 2 b3 4 5 6 7)	ii MODE B DORIAN b2 (1 b2 b3 4 5 6 b7)	III MODE C LYDIAN AUG. (1 2 3 #4 #5 6 7)	IV MODE D LYDIAN DOM. (1 2 3 #4 5 6 b7)	V MODE E HINDU (1 2 3 4 5 b6 b7)	vi MODE F# LOCRIAN ♮2 (1 2 b3 4 b5 b6 b7)	vii MODE G#SUPER LOCRIAN (1 b2 b3 b4 b5 b6 b7)
A^-	B^-	C^+	D	E	$F\#^\circ$	$G\#^\circ$
$A^{SUS\,2}$			$D^{SUS\,2}$	$E^{SUS\,2}$		
A^{SUS}	B^{SUS}			E^{SUS}		
$A^{-\,6}$	$B^{-\,6}$		D^{6}	E^{b6}		
$A^{-\triangle}$	B^{-7}	$C^{\triangle+}$	D^{7}	E^{7}	$F\#^{\varnothing}$	$G\#^{\varnothing}$
$A^{\triangle SUS\,2}$			$D^{7\,SUS\,2}$	$E^{7\,SUS\,2}$		
$A^{\triangle SUS}$	$B^{7\,SUS}$			$E^{7\,SUS}$		
			$D^{7/6}$			
$A^{-\,9/6}$	$B^{-\,9/6}$		$D^{9/6}$			
$A^{-\triangle 9}$	B^{-b9}		D^{9}	E^{9}		
$A^{-\triangle 11}$			$D^{\#11}$	E^{11}		
$A^{-\triangle 13}$			$D^{13\#11}$			

i MODE Bb JAZZ MINOR (1 2 b3 4 5 6 7)	ii MODE C DORIAN b2 (1 b2 b3 4 5 6 b7)	III MODE Db LYDIAN AUG. (1 2 3 #4 #5 6 7)	IV MODE Eb LYDIAN DOM. (1 2 3 #4 5 6 b7)	V MODE F HINDU (1 2 3 4 5 b6 b7)	vi MODE G LOCRIAN ♮2 (1 2 b3 4 b5 b6 b7)	vii MODE A SUPER LOCRIAN (1 b2 b3 b4 b5 b6 b7)
$Bb-$	$C-$	Db^+	Eb	F	$G°$	$A°$
Bb^{SUS2}			Eb^{SUS2}	F^{SUS2}		
Bb^{SUS}	C^{SUS}			F^{SUS}		
$Bb-^6$	$C-^6$		Eb^6	F^{b6}		
$Bb-^\Delta$	$C-^7$	$Db^{\Delta+}$	Eb^7	F^7	G^*	A^*
$Bb^{\Delta SUS2}$			Eb^{7SUS2}	F^{7SUS2}		
$Bb^{\Delta SUS}$	C^{7SUS}			F^{7SUS}		
			$Eb^{7/6}$			
$Bb-^{9/6}$	$C-^{9/6}$		$Eb^{9/6}$			
$Bb-^{\Delta9}$	$C-^{b9}$		Eb^9	F^9		
$Bb-^{\Delta11}$			$Eb^{\#11}$	F^{11}		
$Bb-^{\Delta13}$			$Eb^{13\#11}$			

i MODE B JAZZ MINOR (1 2 b3 4 5 6 7)	ii MODE C# DORIAN b2 (1 b2 b3 4 5 6 b7)	III MODE D LYDIAN AUG. (1 2 3 #4 #5 6 7)	IV MODE E LYDIAN DOM. (1 2 3 #4 5 6 b7)	V MODE F# HINDU (1 2 3 4 5 b6 b7)	vi MODE G# LOCRIAN ♮2 (1 2 b3 4 b5 b6 b7)	vii MODE A# SUPER LOCRIAN (1 b2 b3 b4 b5 b6 b7)
B^{-}	$C\#^{-}$	D^{+}	E	$F\#$	$G\#^{\circ}$	$A\#^{\circ}$
B^{SUS2}			E^{SUS2}	$F\#^{SUS2}$		
B^{SUS}	$C\#^{SUS}$			$F\#^{SUS}$		
B^{-6}	$C\#^{-6}$		E^{6}	$F\#^{b6}$		
$B^{-\triangle}$	$C\#^{-7}$	$D^{\triangle+}$	E^{7}	$F\#^{7}$	$G\#^{ø}$	$A\#^{ø}$
$B^{\triangle SUS2}$			E^{7SUS2}	$F\#^{7SUS2}$		
$B^{\triangle SUS}$	$C\#^{7SUS}$			$F\#^{7SUS}$		
			$E^{7/6}$			
$B^{-9/6}$	$C\#^{-9/6}$		$E^{9/6}$			
$B^{-\triangle 9}$	$C\#^{-b9}$		E^{9}	$F\#^{9}$		
$B^{-\triangle 11}$			$E^{\#11}$	$F\#^{11}$		
$B^{-\triangle 13}$			$E^{13\#11}$			

i MODE C JAZZ MINOR (1 2♭3 4 5 6 7)	ii MODE D DORIAN ♭2 (1♭2♭3 4 5 6♭7)	iii MODE E♭ LYDIAN AUG. (1 2 3♯4♯5 6 7)	IV MODE F LYDIAN DOM. (1 2 3♯4 5 6♭7)	V MODE G HINDU (1 2 3 4 5 ♭6♭7)	vi MODE A LOCRIAN ♮2 (1 2 ♭3 4♭5♭6♭7)	vii MODE B SUPER LOCRIAN (1♭2♭3♭4♭5♭6♭7)
C^{-}	D^{-}	$E♭^{+}$	F	G	A°	B°
C^{sus2}			F^{sus2}	G^{sus2}		
C^{sus}	D^{sus}			G^{sus}		
C^{-6}	D^{-6}		F^{6}	$G^{♭6}$		
$C^{-\triangle}$	D^{-7}	$E♭^{\triangle+}$	F^{7}	G^{7}	$A^{\varnothing}$	$B^{\varnothing}$
$C^{\triangle sus2}$			F^{7sus2}	G^{7sus2}		
$C^{\triangle sus}$	D^{7sus}			G^{7sus}		
			$F^{7/6}$			
$C^{-9/6}$	$D^{-9/6}$		$F^{9/6}$			
$C^{-\triangle 9}$	$D^{-♭9}$		F^{9}	G^{9}		
$C^{-\triangle 11}$			$F^{\sharp 11}$	G^{11}		
$C^{-\triangle 13}$			$F^{13\sharp 11}$			

THE MATRIX

i MODE Db JAZZ MINOR (1 2 b3 4 5 6 7)	ii MODE Eb DORIAN b2 (1 b2 b3 4 5 6 b7)	III MODE Fb LYDIAN AUG. (1 2 3 #4 #5 6 7)	IV MODE Gb LYDIAN DOM. (1 2 3 #4 5 6 b7)	V MODE Ab HINDU (1 2 3 4 5 b6 b7)	vi MODE B LOCRIAN ♮2 (1 2 b3 4 b5 b6 b7)	vii MODE C SUPER LOCRIAN (1 b2 b3 b4 b5 b6 b7)
Db−	Eb−	Fb+	Gb	Ab	Bb°	C°
Db sus2			Gb sus2	Ab sus2		
Db sus	Eb sus			Ab sus		
Db−6	Eb−6		Gb6	Ab b6		
Db−△	Eb−7	Fb△+	Gb7	Ab7	Bb ø	C ø
Db△sus2			Gb7sus2	Ab7sus2		
Db△sus	Eb7sus			Ab7sus		
			Gb7/6			
Db−9/6	Eb−9/6		Gb9/6			
Db△9	Eb−b9		Gb9	Ab9		
Db△11			Gb#11	Ab11		
Db△13			Gb13#11			

69

i MODE D JAZZ MINOR (1 2 b3 4 5 6 7)	ii MODE E DORIAN b2 (1 b2 b3 4 5 6 b7)	III MODE F LYDIAN AUG. (1 2 3 #4 #5 6 7)	IV MODE G LYDIAN DOM. (1 2 3 #4 5 6 b7)	V MODE A HINDU (1 2 3 4 5 b6 b7)	vi MODE B LOCRIAN ♮2 (1 2 b3 4 b5 b6 b7)	vii MODE C# SUPER LOCRIAN (1 b2 b3 b4 b5 b6 b7)
D^{-}	E^{-}	F^{+}	G	A	B°	$C\#^{\circ}$
D^{sus2}			G^{sus2}	A^{sus2}		
D^{sus}	E^{sus}			A^{sus}		
D^{-6}	E^{-6}		G^{6}	$A^{\flat 6}$		
$D^{-\triangle}$	E^{-7}	$F^{\triangle +}$	G^{7}	A^{7}	$B^{\varnothing}$	$C\#^{\varnothing}$
$D^{\triangle sus2}$			G^{7sus2}	A^{7sus2}		
$D^{\triangle sus}$	E^{7sus}			A^{7sus}		
			$G^{7/6}$			
$D^{-9/6}$	$E^{-9/6}$		$G^{9/6}$			
$D^{-\triangle 9}$	$E^{-\flat 9}$		G^{9}	A^{9}		
$D^{-\triangle 11}$			$G^{\#11}$	A^{11}		
$D^{-\triangle 13}$			$G^{13\#11}$			

THE MATRIX

i MODE Eb JAZZ MINOR (1 2b3 4 5 6 7)	ii MODE F DORIAN b2 (1 b2 b3 4 5 6 b7)	III MODE Gb LYDIAN AUG. (1 2 3 #4 #5 6 7)	IV MODE Ab LYDIAN DOM. (1 2 3 #4 5 6 b7)	V MODE Bb HINDU (1 2 3 4 5 b6 b7)	vi MODE C LOCRIAN ♮2 (1 2 b3 4 b5 b6 b7)	vii MODE D SUPER LOCRIAN (1 b2 b3 b4 b5 b6 b7)
Eb–	F –	Gb+	Ab	Bb	C °	D °
Eb sus2			Ab sus2	Bb sus2		
Eb sus	F sus			Bb sus		
Eb–6	F–6		Ab6	Bb b6		
Eb–△	F–7	Gb△+	Ab7	Bb7	C ø	D ø
Eb △sus2			Ab 7sus2	Bb 7sus2		
Eb △sus	F 7sus			Bb 7sus		
			Ab 7/6			
Eb–9/6	F–9/6		Ab 9/6			
Eb–△9	F–b9		Ab9	Bb9		
Eb–△11			Ab#11	Bb11		
Eb–△13			Ab13#11			

i MODE E JAZZ MINOR (1 2 b3 4 5 6 7)	ii MODE F# DORIAN b2 (1 b2 b3 4 5 6 b7)	III MODE G LYDIAN AUG. (1 2 3 #4 5 6 7)	IV MODE A LYDIAN DOM. (1 2 3 #4 5 6 b7)	V MODE B HINDU (1 2 3 4 5 b6 b7)	vi MODE C# LOCRIAN ♮2 (1 2 b3 4 b5 b6 b7)	vii MODE D# SUPER LOCRIAN (1 b2 b3 b4 b5 b6 b7)
E -	F# -	G $^+$	A	B	C# °	D# °
E $^{SUS\,2}$			A $^{SUS\,2}$	B $^{SUS\,2}$		
E ^{SUS}	F# ^{SUS}			B ^{SUS}		
E- ^{6}	F#- ^{6}		A ^{6}	B ^{b6}		
E- $^\triangle$	F#- ^{7}	G $^{\triangle+}$	A ^{7}	B ^{7}	C# $^\varnothing$	D# $^\varnothing$
E $^{\triangle\,SUS\,2}$			A $^{7\,SUS\,2}$	B $^{7\,SUS\,2}$		
E $^{\triangle\,SUS}$	F# $^{7\,SUS}$			B $^{7\,SUS}$		
			A $^{7/6}$			
E- $^{9/6}$	F#- $^{9/6}$		A $^{9/6}$			
E- $^{\triangle 9}$	F#- ^{b9}		A ^{9}	B ^{9}		
E- $^{\triangle 11}$			A $^{\#11}$	B ^{11}		
E- $^{\triangle 13}$			A $^{13\#11}$			

THE HARMONIC MINOR

i MODE - F HARMONIC MINOR

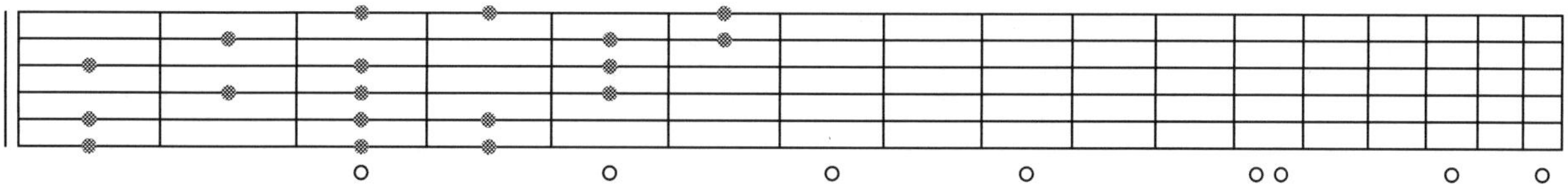

BASIC TRIAD - F MINOR (1♭3 5)

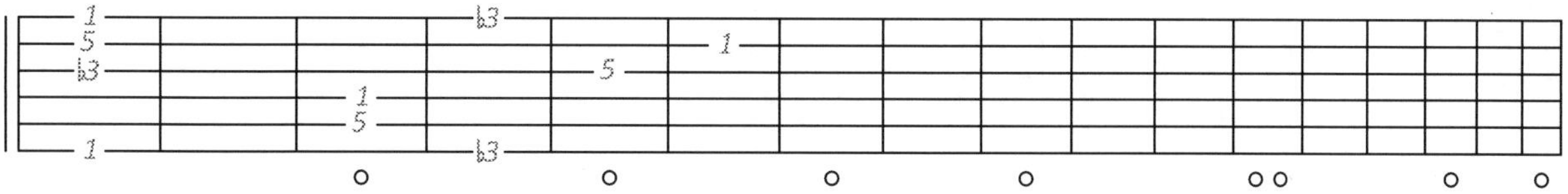

F SUS 2 (1 2 5)

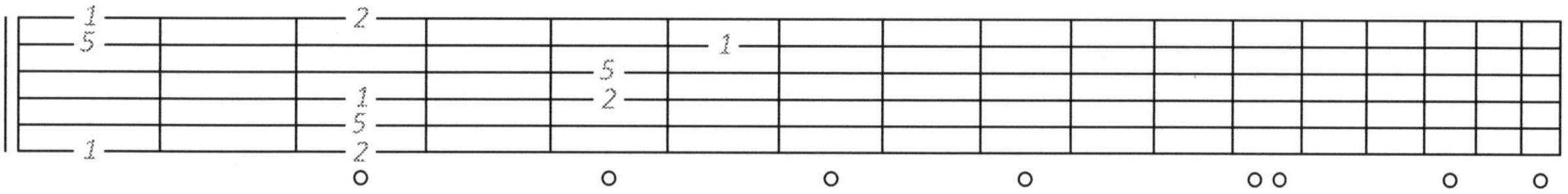

F SUS (1 4 5)

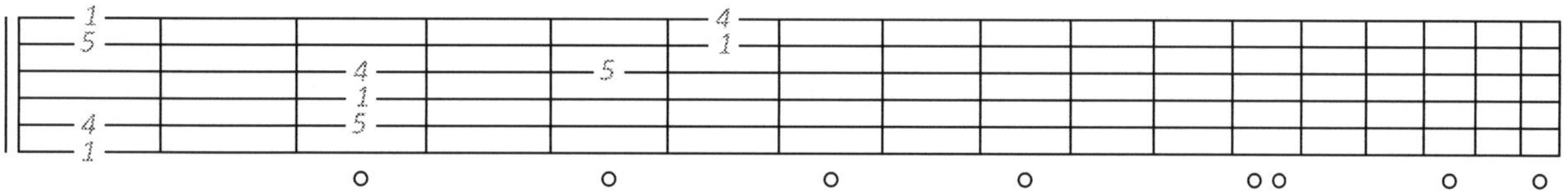

F MINOR FLAT SIX (1♭3 5 ♭6)

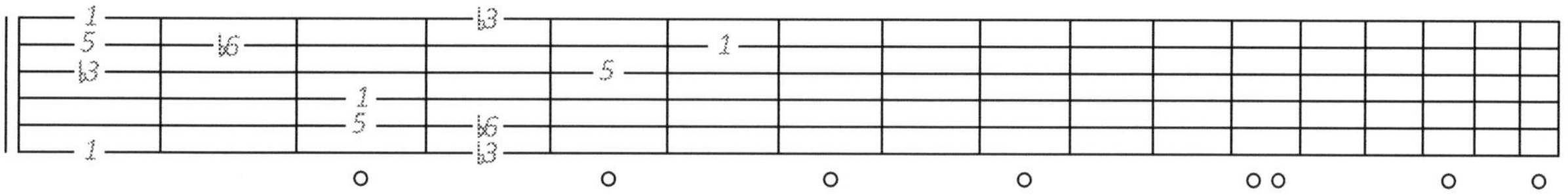

F MINOR MAJOR SEVENTH (1♭3 5 7)

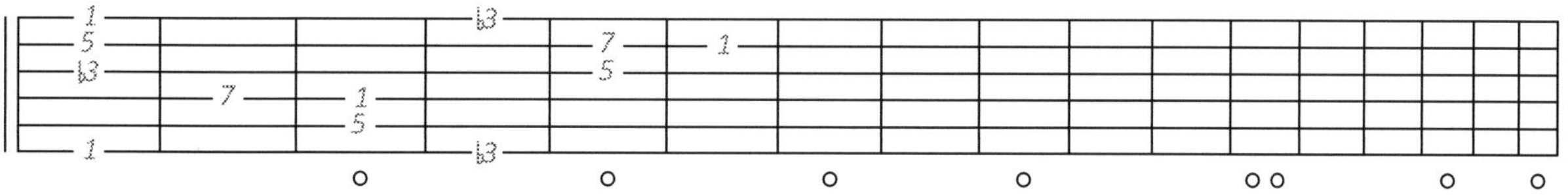

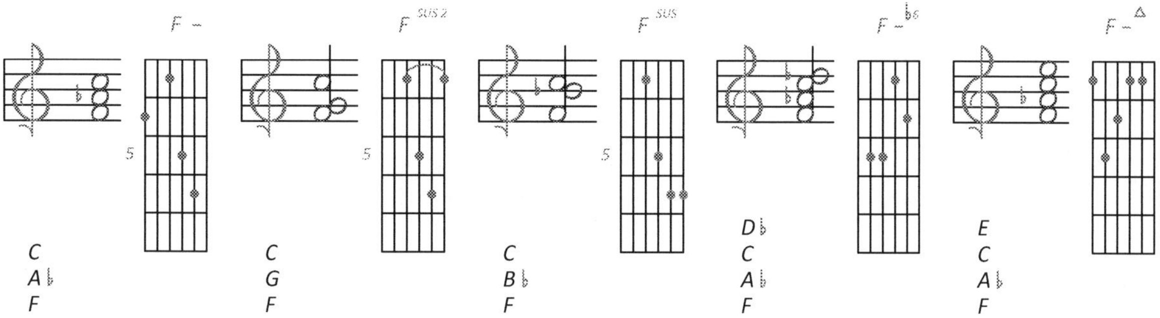

ARPEGGIO OPTIONS

F ⁻   F ˢᵘˢ²   F ˢᵘˢ   F ⁻♭⁶   F ⁻ᐃ

C
A♭
F

C
G
F

C
B♭
F

D♭
C
A♭
F

E
C
A♭
F

i MODE - F HARMONIC MINOR

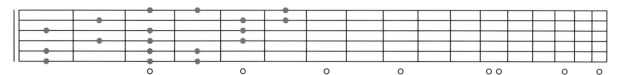

F MAJOR SEVENTH SUS 2 (1 2 5 7)

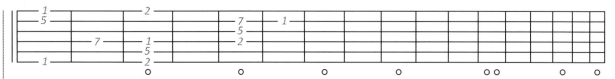

F MAJOR SEVENTH SUS (1 4 5 7)

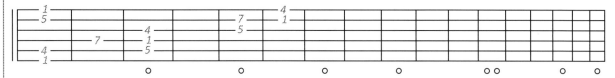

F MINOR MAJOR NINTH (1 ♭3 5 7 9)

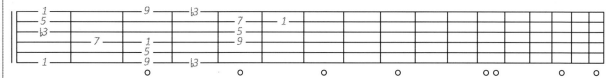

F MINOR MAJOR ELEVENTH (1 ♭3 5 7 9 11)

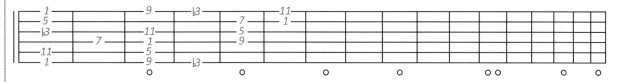

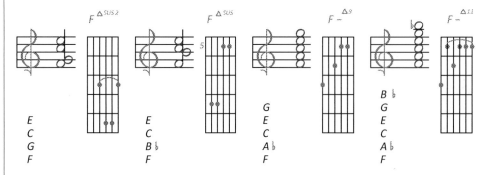

ii MODE
G LOCRIAN ♮6 (1♭2♭3 4♭5 6♭7)

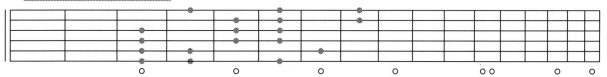

BASIC TRIAD G DIMINISHED (1♭3♭5)

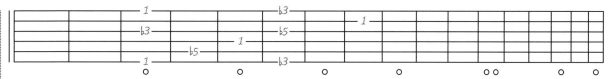

G HALF DIMINISHED SEVENTH (1♭3♭5♭7)

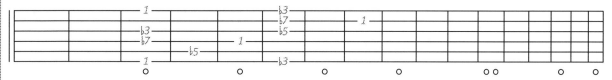

ARPEGGIO OPTIONS

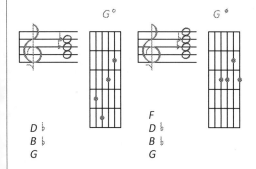

G°

G °

D ♭
B ♭
G

F
D ♭
B ♭
G

III MODE
A♭ IONIAN #5 (1 2 3 4 #5 6 7)

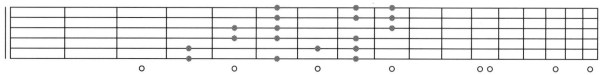

BASIC TRIAD A♭ AUGMENTED (1 3 #5)

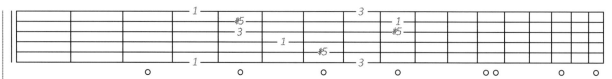

A♭ MAJOR SEVENTH AUGMENTED (1 3 #5 7)

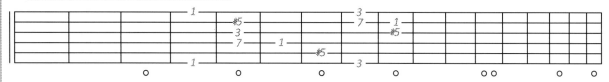

ARPEGGIO OPTIONS

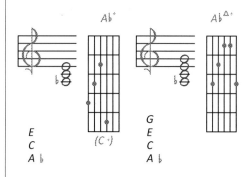

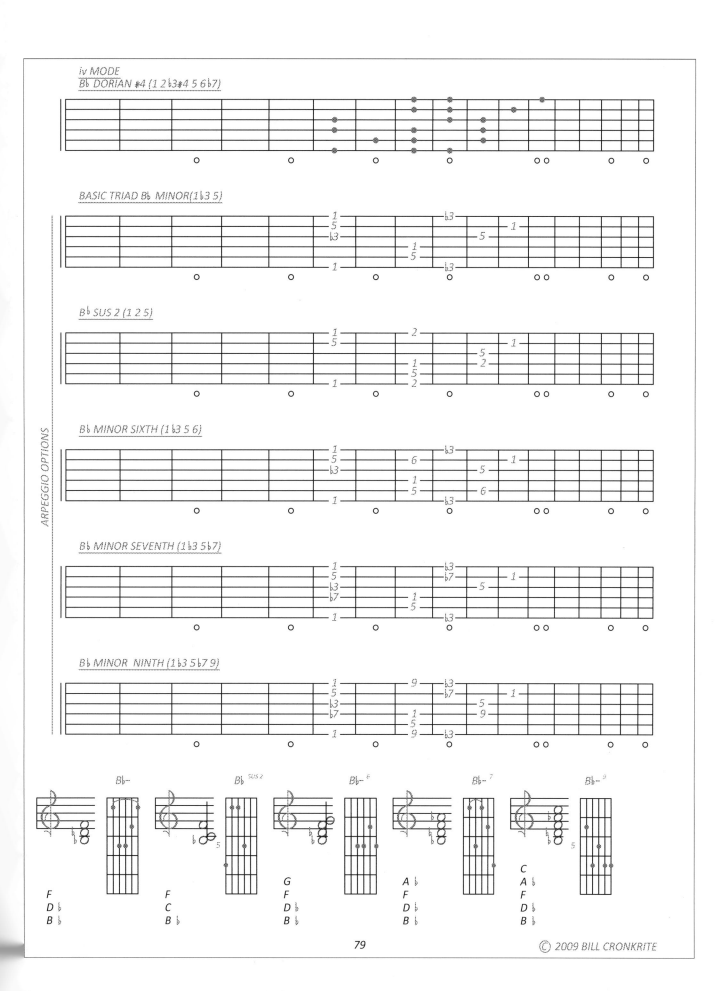

iv MODE
Bb DORIAN #4 (1 2 b3 #4 5 6 b7)

Bb MINOR SHARP ELEVEN(1 b3 5 b7 9 #11)

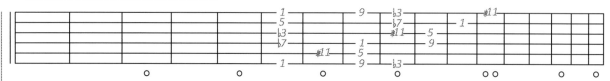

Bb MINOR THIRTEENTH SHARP ELEVEN(1 b3 5 b7 9 #11 13)

ARPEGGIO OPTIONS

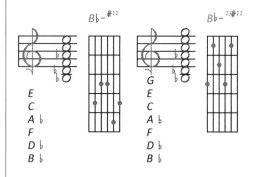

80

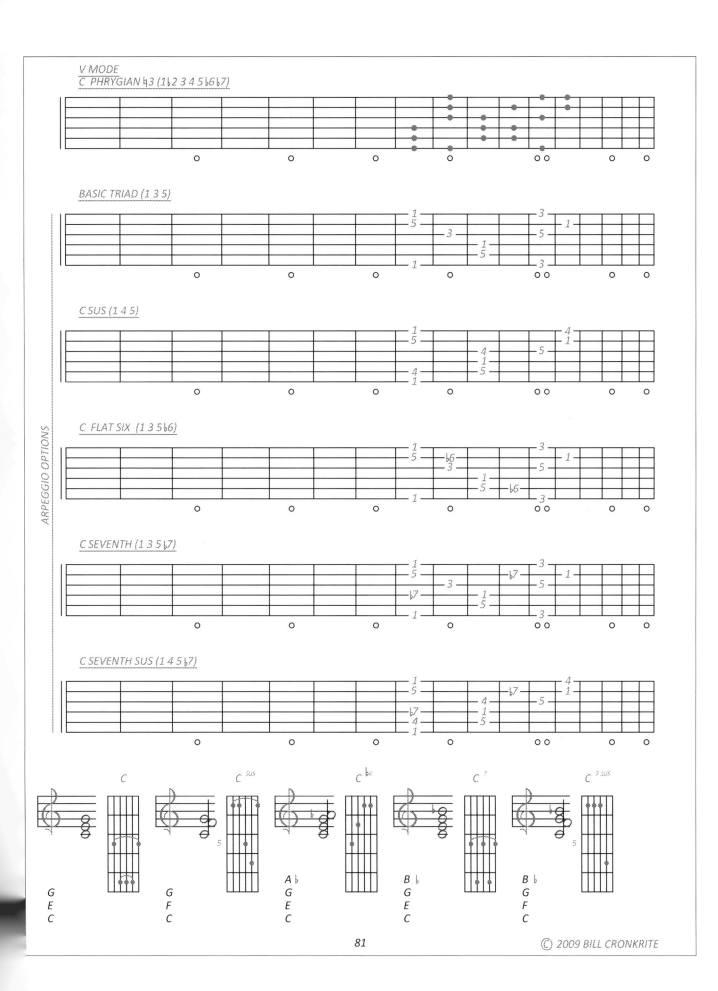

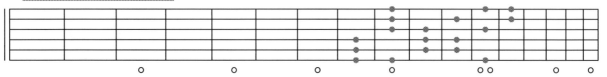

V MODE
C PHRYGIAN ♮3 (1 ♭2 3 4 5 ♭6 ♭7)

C FLAT NINE (1 3 5 ♭7 ♭9)

ARPEGGIO OPTIONS

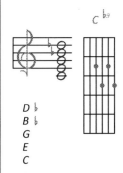

C ♭9

D ♭
B ♭
G
E
C

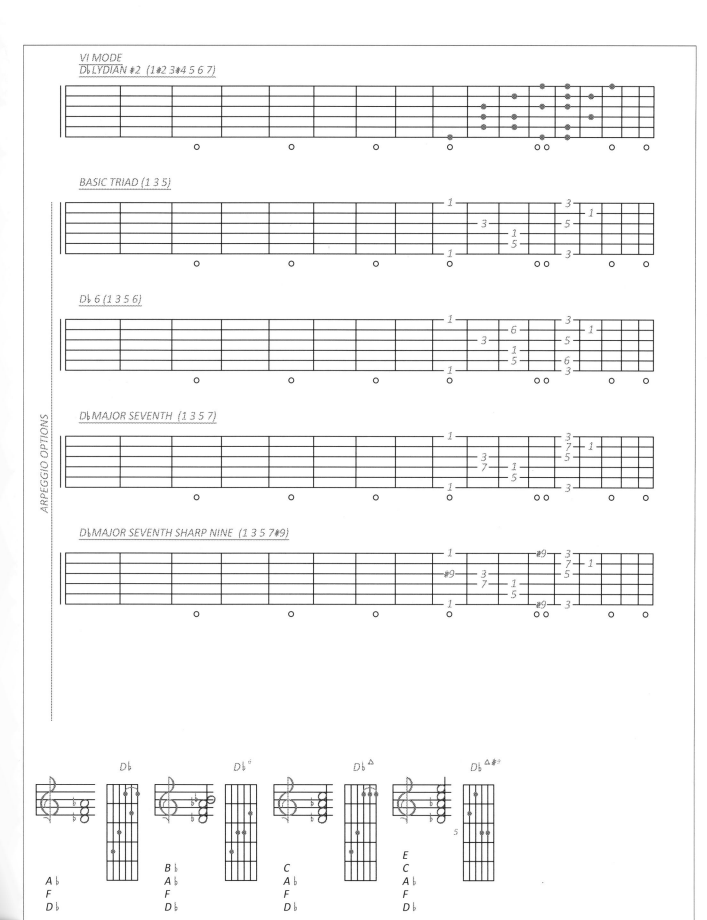

vii MODE
(1♭2♭3♭4♭5♭6♭♭7)

BASIC TRIAD (1♭3♭5)

E HALF DIMINISHED SEVENTH (1♭3♭5♭♭7)

ARPEGGIO OPTIONS

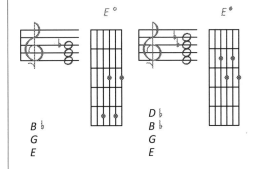

E °
E ⌀

B♭
G
E

D♭
B♭
G
E

i MODE F HARMONIC MIN (1 2 b3 4 5 b6 7)	ii MODE G LOCRIAN ♮6 (1 b2 b3 4 b5 6 b7)	III MODE Ab IONIAN #5 (1 2 3 4 #5 6 7)	iv MODE Bb DORIAN #4 (1 2 b3 #4 5 6 b7)	V MODE C PHRYGIAN ♮3 (1 b2 3 4 5 b6 b7)	VI MODE Db LYDIAN #2 (1 #2 3 #4 5 6 7)	vii MODE (1 b2 b3 4 b5 b6 bb7)
F −	G °	Ab +	Bb −	C	Db	E °
F SUS 2			Bb SUS 2			
F SUS				C SUS		
F −b6			Bb −6	C b6	Db 6	
F −△	G ø	Ab △+	Bb −7	C 7	Db △	E °7
F △SUS 2						
F △SUS				C 7 SUS		
F −△9			Bb −9	C b9	Db △#9	
F −△11			Bb −#11			
			Bb −13#11			

THE MATRIX

i MODE F# HARMONIC MIN (1 2 b3 4 5 b6 7)	ii MODE G# LOCRIAN ♮6 (1 b2 b3 4 b5 6 b7)	III MODE A IONIAN #5 (1 2 3 4 #5 6 7)	iv MODE B DORIAN #4 (1 2 b3 #4 5 6 b7)	V MODE C# PHRYGIAN ♮3 (1 b2 3 4 5 b6 b7)	VI MODE D LYDIAN #2 (1 #2 3 #4 5 6 7)	vii MODE (1 b2 b3 b4 b5 b6 bb7)
$F\#-$	$G\#°$	A^+	$B-$	$C\#$	D	$E\#°$
$F\#^{SUS\,2}$			$B^{SUS\,2}$			
$F\#^{SUS}$				$C\#^{SUS}$		
$F\#-^{\flat\,6}$			$B-^{6}$	$C\#^{\flat 6}$	D^{6}	
$F\#-^{\triangle}$	$G\#^{ø}$	$A^{\triangle+}$	$B-^{7}$	$C\#^{7}$	$D^{\triangle}$	$E\#^{°7}$
$F\#^{\triangle SUS\,2}$						
$F\#^{\triangle SUS}$				$C\#^{7\,SUS}$		
$F\#-^{\triangle\,9}$			$B-^{9}$	$C\#^{\flat 9}$	$D^{\triangle \#9}$	
$F\#-^{\triangle\,11}$			$B-^{\#\,11}$			
			$B-^{13\#11}$			

i MODE G HARMONIC MIN $(1\ 2\ b3\ 4\ 5\ b6\ 7)$	ii MODE A LOCRIAN ♮6 $(1\ b2\ b3\ 4\ b5\ 6\ b7)$	III MODE Bb IONIAN #5 $(1\ 2\ 3\ 4\ \#5\ 6\ 7)$	iv MODE C DORIAN #4 $(1\ 2\ b3\ \#4\ 5\ 6\ b7)$	V MODE D PHRYGIAN ♮3 $(1\ b2\ 3\ 4\ 5\ b6\ b7)$	VI MODE Eb LYDIAN #2 $(1\ \#2\ 3\ \#4\ 5\ 6\ 7)$	vii MODE $(1\ b2\ b3\ b4\ b5\ b6\ bb7)$
$G\,-$	$A\,°$	$Bb\,^+$	$C\,-$	D	Eb	$F\#\,°$
$G^{SUS\,2}$			$C^{SUS\,2}$			
G^{SUS}				D^{SUS}		
$G-^{b6}$			$C-^{6}$	D^{b6}	Eb^{6}	
$G-^{\triangle}$	$A^{\o}$	$Bb^{\triangle+}$	$C-^{7}$	D^{7}	$Eb^{\triangle}$	$F\#^{°7}$
$G^{\triangle SUS\,2}$						
$G^{\triangle SUS}$				$D^{7\,SUS}$		
$G-^{\triangle\,9}$			$C-^{9}$	D^{b9}	$Eb^{\triangle\#9}$	
$G-^{\triangle\,11}$			$C-^{\#11}$			
			$C-^{13\#11}$			

i MODE Ab HARMONIC MIN (1 2 b3 4 5 b6 7)	ii MODE Bb LOCRIAN ♮6 (1 b2 b3 4 b5 6 b7)	III MODE Cb IONIAN #5 (1 2 3 4 #5 6 7)	iv MODE Db DORIAN #4 (1 2 b3 #4 5 6 b7)	V MODE Eb PHRYGIAN ♮3 (1 b2 3 4 5 b6 b7)	VI MODE Fb LYDIAN #2 (1 #2 3 #4 5 6 7)	vii MODE (1 b2 b3 b4 b5 b6 bb7)
Ab −	Bb °	Cb +	Db −	Eb	Fb	G °
Ab $^{SUS\,2}$			Db $^{SUS\,2}$			
Ab ^{SUS}				Eb ^{SUS}		
Ab− $^{b\,6}$			Db− ^{6}	Eb ^{b6}	Fb ^{6}	
Ab− $^{\triangle}$	Bb ^{ø}	Cb $^{\triangle+}$	Db− ^{7}	Eb ^{7}	Fb $^{\triangle}$	G $^{°7}$
Ab $^{\triangle SUS\,2}$						
Ab $^{\triangle SUS}$				Eb $^{7\,SUS}$		
Ab− $^{\triangle\,9}$			Db− ^{9}	Eb ^{b9}	Fb $^{\triangle\#9}$	
Ab− $^{\triangle\,11}$			Db− $^{\#\,11}$			
			Db− $^{13\#\,11}$			

i MODE A HARMONIC MIN (1 2 b3 4 5 b6 7)	ii MODE B LOCRIAN ♮6 (1 b2 b3 4 b5 6 b7)	III MODE C IONIAN #5 (1 2 3 4 #5 6 7)	iv MODE D DORIAN #4 (1 2 b3 #4 5 6 b7)	V MODE E PHRYGIAN ♮3 (1 b2 3 4 5 b6 b7)	VI MODE F LYDIAN #2 (1 #2 3 #4 5 6 7)	vii MODE (1 b2 b3 b4 b5 b6 bb7)
$A-$	$B°$	C^+	$D-$	E	F	$G\#°$
$A^{SUS\,2}$			$D^{SUS\,2}$			
A^{SUS}				E^{SUS}		
$A-^{b6}$			$D-^{6}$	E^{b6}	F^{6}	
$A-^{\triangle}$	$B^{\varnothing}$	$C^{\triangle+}$	$D-^{7}$	E^{7}	$F^{\triangle}$	$G\#^{°7}$
$A^{\triangle SUS\,2}$						
$A^{\triangle SUS}$				$E^{7\,SUS}$		
$A-^{\triangle 9}$			$D-^{9}$	E^{b9}	$F^{\triangle\#9}$	
$A-^{\triangle 11}$			$D-^{\#11}$			
			$D-^{13\#11}$			

i MODE Bb HARMONIC MIN (1 2 b3 4 5 b6 7)	ii MODE C LOCRIAN ♮6 (1 b2 b3 4 b5 6 b7)	III MODE Db IONIAN #5 (1 2 3 4 #5 6 7)	iv MODE Eb DORIAN #4 (1 2 b3 #4 5 6 b7)	V MODE F PHRYGIAN ♮3 (1 b2 3 4 5 b6 b7)	VI MODE Gb LYDIAN #2 (1 #2 3 #4 5 6 7)	vii MODE (1 b2 b3 b4 b5 b6 bb7)
Bb −	C °	Db +	Eb −−	F	Gb	A °
Bb SUS 2			Eb SUS 2			
Bb SUS				F SUS		
Bb −b6			Eb −6	F b6	Gb 6	
Bb −Δ	C *	Db Δ+	Eb −7	F 7	Gb Δ	A °7
Bb ΔSUS 2						
Bb ΔSUS				F 7SUS		
Bb −Δ9			Eb −9	F b9	Gb Δ#9	
Bb −Δ11			Eb −#11			
			Eb −13#11			

90

THE MATRIX

i MODE B HARMONIC MIN (1 2 b3 4 5 b6 7)	ii MODE C# LOCRIAN ♮6 (1 b2 b3 4 b5 6 b7)	III MODE D IONIAN #5 (1 2 3 4 #5 6 7)	iv MODE E DORIAN #4 (1 2 b3 #4 5 6 b7)	V MODE F# PHRYGIAN ♮3 (1 b2 3 4 5 b6 b7)	VI MODE G LYDIAN #2 (1 #2 3 #4 5 6 7)	vii MODE (1 b2 b3 b4 b5 b6 bb7)
B -	C#°	D⁺	E -	F#	G	A#°
B $^{SUS\,2}$			E $^{SUS\,2}$			
B ^{SUS}				F# ^{SUS}		
B - ^{b6}			E - ^{6}	F# ^{b6}	G ^{6}	
B - $^{\triangle}$	C# ^{ø}	D $^{\triangle+}$	E - ^{7}	F# ^{7}	G $^{\triangle}$	A# $^{°7}$
B $^{\triangle SUS\,2}$						
B $^{\triangle SUS}$				F# $^{7\,SUS}$		
B - $^{\triangle\,9}$			E - ^{9}	F# ^{b9}	G $^{\triangle\#9}$	
B - $^{\triangle\,11}$			E - $^{\#\,11}$			
			E - $^{13\#\,11}$			

i MODE C HARMONIC MIN (1 2 b3 4 5 b6 7)	ii MODE D LOCRIAN ♮6 (1 b2 b3 4 b5 6 b7)	III MODE Eb IONIAN #5 (1 2 3 4 #5 6 7)	iv MODE F DORIAN #4 (1 2 b3 #4 5 6 b7)	V MODE G PHRYGIAN ♮3 (1 b2 3 4 5 b6 b7)	VI MODE Ab LYDIAN #2 (1 #2 3 #4 5 6 7)	vii MODE (1 b2 b3 b4 b5 b6 bb7)
C −	D °	Eb +	F −	G	Ab	B °
C sus2			F sus2			
C sus				G sus		
C −b6			F −6	G b6	Ab 6	
C −Δ	D #	Eb Δ+	F −7	G 7	Ab Δ	B °7
C ΔSUS2						
C ΔSUS				G 7SUS		
C −Δ9			F −9	G b9	Ab Δ#9	
C −Δ11			F −#11			
			F −13#11			

92

THE MATRIX

i MODE C# HARMONIC MIN (1 2 b3 4 5 b6 7)	ii MODE D# LOCRIAN ♮6 (1 b2 b3 4 b5 6 b7)	III MODE E IONIAN #5 (1 2 3 4 #5 6 7)	iv MODE F# DORIAN #4 (1 2 b3 #4 5 6 b7)	V MODE G# PHRYGIAN ♮3 (1 b2 3 4 5 b6 b7)	VI MODE A LYDIAN #2 (1 #2 3 #4 5 6 7)	vii MODE (1 b2 b3 b4 b5 b6 bb7)
C# −	D#°	E +	F#−	G#	A	B# °
C# SUS 2			F# SUS 2			
C# SUS				G# SUS		
C#− b6			F#− 6	G# b6	A 6	
C#−△	D#ø	E △+	F#− 7	G# 7	A △	B# °7
C# △SUS 2						
C# △SUS				G# 7 SUS		
C#−△ 9			F#− 9	G# b9	A △#9	
C#−△ 11			F#− #11			
			F#− 13 #11			

93

i MODE D HARMONIC MIN (1 2 b3 4 5 b6 7)	ii MODE E LOCRIAN ♮6 (1 b2 b3 4 b5 6 b7)	III MODE F IONIAN #5 (1 2 3 4 #5 6 7)	iv MODE G DORIAN #4 (1 2 b3 #4 5 6 b7)	V MODE A PHRYGIAN ♮3 (1 b2 3 4 5 b6 b7)	VI MODE Bb LYDIAN #2 (1 #2 3 #4 5 6 7)	vii MODE (1 b2 b3 b4 b5 b6 bb7)
$D-$	$E°$	F^+	$G-$	A	$B\flat$	$C\#°$
$D^{SUS\,2}$			$G^{SUS\,2}$			
D^{SUS}				A^{SUS}		
$D-^{\flat 6}$			$G-^{6}$	$A^{\flat 6}$	$B\flat^{6}$	
$D-^{\triangle}$	$E^{\#}$	$F^{\triangle +}$	$G-^{7}$	A^{7}	$B\flat^{\triangle}$	$C\#^{°7}$
$D^{\triangle SUS\,2}$						
$D^{\triangle SUS}$				$A^{7\,SUS}$		
$D-^{\triangle 9}$			$G-^{9}$	$A^{\flat 9}$	$B\flat^{\triangle \#9}$	
$D-^{\triangle 11}$			$G-^{\#11}$			
			$G-^{13\#11}$			

THE MATRIX

i MODE Eb HARMONIC MIN (1 2 b3 4 5 b6 7)	ii MODE F LOCRIAN ♮6 (1 b2 b3 4 b5 6 b7)	III MODE Gb IONIAN #5 (1 2 3 4 #5 6 7)	iv MODE Ab DORIAN #4 (1 2 b3 #4 5 6 b7)	V MODE Bb PHRYGIAN ♮3 (1 b2 3 4 5 b6 b7)	VI MODE Cb LYDIAN #2 (1 #2 3 4 5 6 7)	vii MODE (1 b2 b3 b4 b5 b6 bb7)
Eb −	F °	Gb +	Ab −	Bb	Cb	D °
Eb SUS2			Ab SUS2			
Eb SUS				Bb SUS		
Eb −b6			Ab −6	Bb b6	Cb 6	
Eb −Δ	F ø	Gb Δ+	Ab −7	Bb 7	Cb Δ	D °7
Eb ΔSUS2						
Eb ΔSUS				Bb 7SUS		
Eb −Δ9			Ab −9	Bb b9	Cb Δ#9	
Eb −Δ11			Ab −#11			
			Ab −13#11			

95

i MODE E HARMONIC MIN (1 2 b3 4 5 b6 7)	ii MODE F# LOCRIAN ♮6 (1 b2 b3 4 b5 6 b7)	III MODE G IONIAN #5 (1 2 3 4 #5 6 7)	iv MODE A DORIAN #4 (1 2 b3 #4 5 6 b7)	V MODE B PHRYGIAN ♮3 (1 b2 3 4 5 b6 b7)	VI MODE C LYDIAN #2 (1 #2 3 #4 5 6 7)	vii MODE (1 b2 b3 b4 b5 b6 bb7)
E −	F#°	G +	A −	B	C	D#°
E sus2			A sus2			
E sus5				B sus		
E − b6			A − 6	B b6	C 6	
E − △	F#°	G △+	A − 7	B 7	C △	D#° 7
E △sus2						
E △sus				B 7sus		
E − △ 9			A − 9	B b9	C △#9	
E − △ 11			A − #11			
			A − 13#11			

96

THE HARMONIC MAJOR

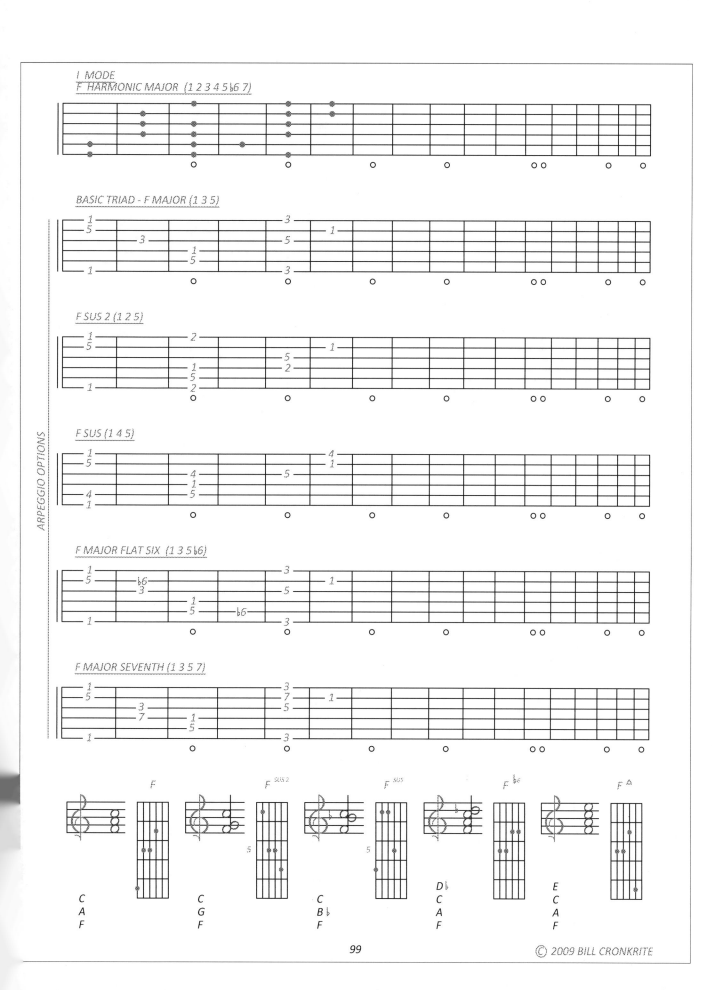

I MODE
F HARMONIC MAJOR (1 2 3 4 5 ♭6 7)

BASIC TRIAD - F MAJOR (1 3 5)

F SUS 2 (1 2 5)

F SUS (1 4 5)

F MAJOR FLAT SIX (1 3 5 ♭6)

F MAJOR SEVENTH (1 3 5 7)

ARPEGGIO OPTIONS

I MODE
F HARMONIC MAJOR (1 2 3 4 5♭6 7)

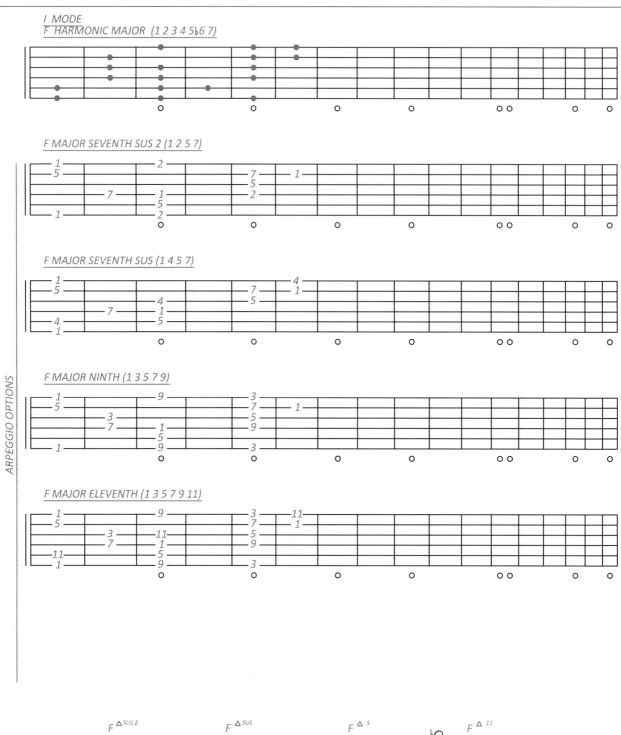

F MAJOR SEVENTH SUS 2 (1 2 5 7)

F MAJOR SEVENTH SUS (1 4 5 7)

F MAJOR NINTH (1 3 5 7 9)

F MAJOR ELEVENTH (1 3 5 7 9 11)

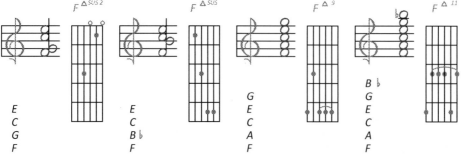

F △SUS 2

E
C
G
F

F △SUS

E
C
B♭
F

F △9

G
E
C
A
F

F △9

B♭
G
E
C
A
F

F △11

ii MODE
G DORIAN ♭5 (1 2 ♭3 4 ♭5 6 ♭7)

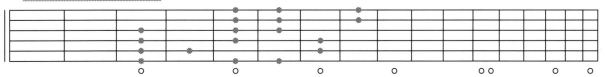

BASIC TRIAD G DIMINISHED (1 ♭3 ♭5)

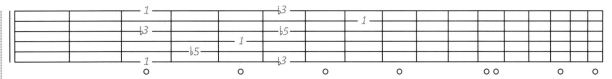

G HALF DIMINISHED SEVENTH (1 ♭3 ♭5 ♭7)

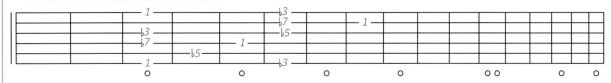

ARPEGGIO OPTIONS

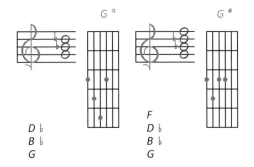

G °   G ⌀

D ♮
B ♭
G

F ♮
D ♮
B ♭
G

101

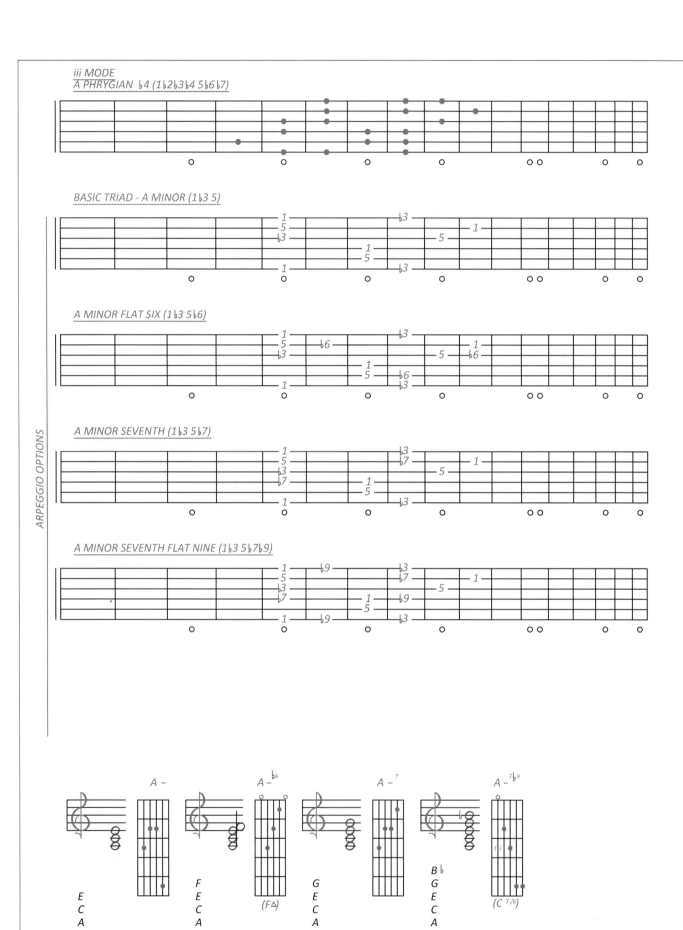

102

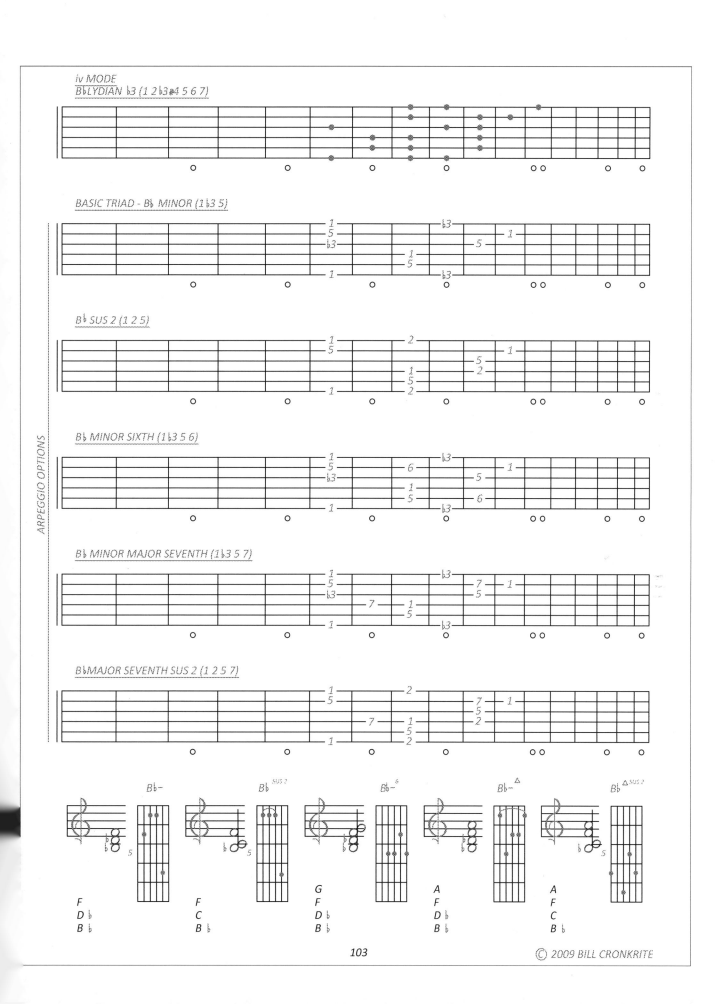

ARPEGGIO OPTIONS

iv MODE
Bb LYDIAN b3 (1 2 b3 #4 5 6 7)

Bb MINOR NINE/SIX (1 b3 5 6 9)

Bb MINOR MAJOR NINTH (1 b3 5 7 9)

Bb MINOR MAJOR NINTH SHARP ELEVEN (1 b3 5 7 9 #11)

Bb MINOR MAJOR THIRTEENTH SHARP ELEVEN (1 b3 5 7 9 #11 13)

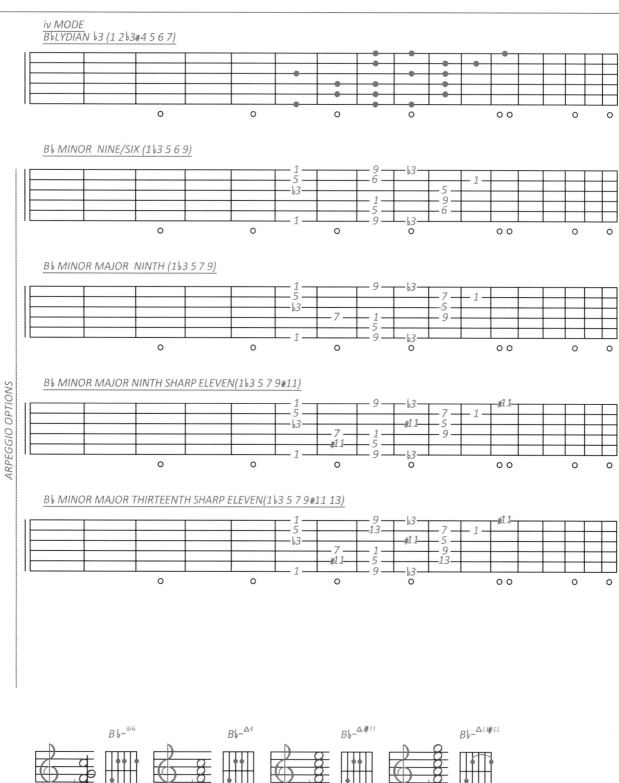

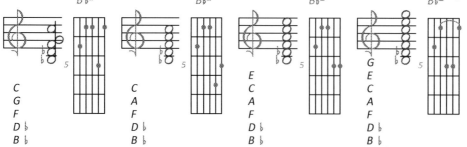

$Bb-^{9/6}$ $Bb-^{\triangle 9}$ $Bb-^{\triangle \#11}$ $Bb-^{\triangle 13 \#11}$

C	C	E	G
G	A	C	E
F	F	A	C
Db	Db	F	A
Bb	Bb	Db	F
		Bb	Db
			Bb

104

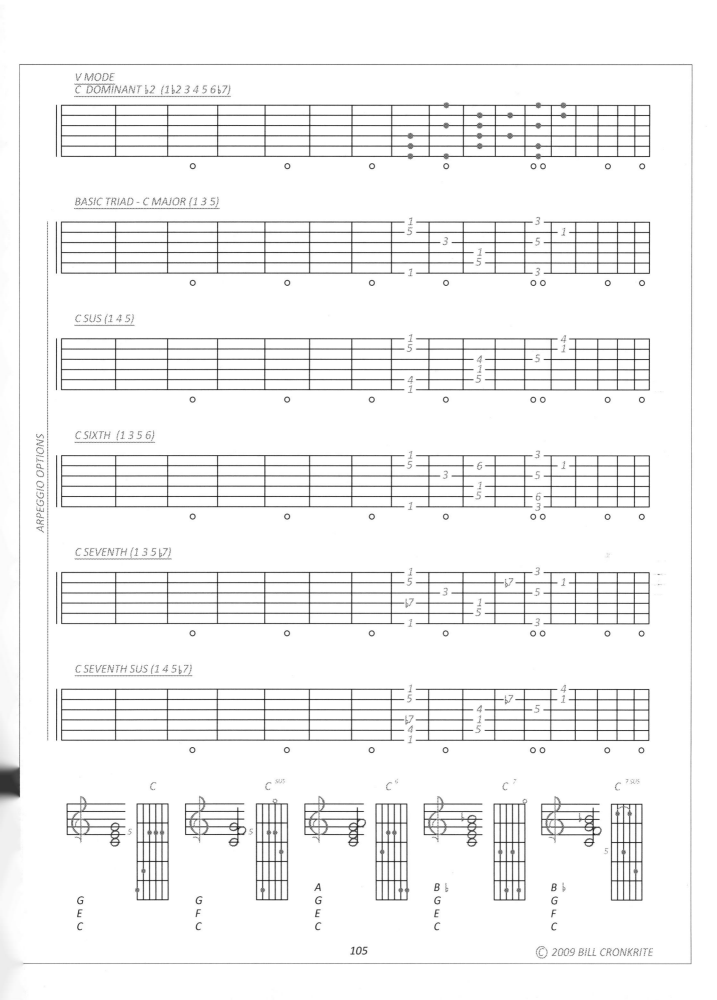

V MODE
C DOMINANT ♭2 (1 ♭2 3 4 5 6 ♭7)

C SEVEN/SIX (1 3 5 6 ♭7)

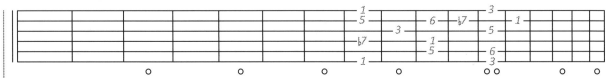

C FLAT NINE (1 3 5 ♭7 ♭9)

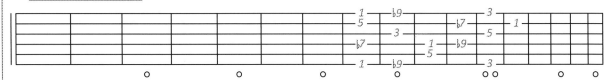

ARPEGGIO OPTIONS

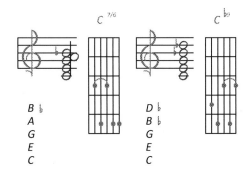

VI MODE
Dᵇ LYDIAN AUGMENTED #2 (1 #2 3 #4 #5 6 7)

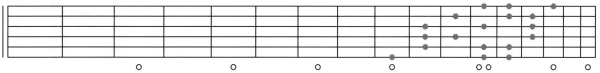

BASIC TRIAD - Dᵇ AUGMENTED(1 3 #5)

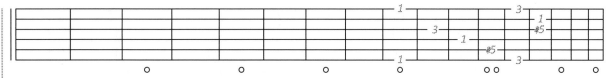

Dᵇ MAJOR SEVENTH SHARP 5(1 3 #5 7)

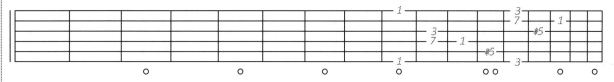

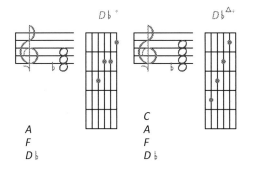

107

vii MODE
E LOCRIAN ♭♭7(1♭2♭3 4♭5♭6♭♭7)

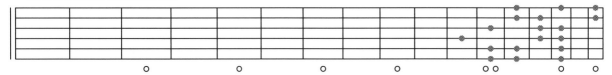

BASIC TRIAD - E DIMINISHED(1♭3♭5)

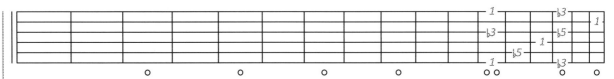

E DIMINISHED SEVENTH (1♭3♭5♭♭7)

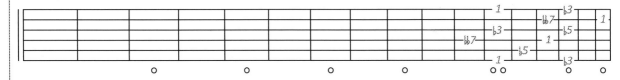

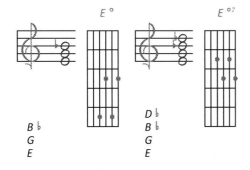

E°   E°7

B♭   D♭
G   B♭
E   G
      E

© 2009 BILL CRONKRITE

I MODE F HARMONIC MAJ (1 2 3 4 5 $\flat$6 7)	ii MODE G DORIAN $\flat$5 (1 2 $\flat$3 4 $\flat$5 6 $\flat$7)	iii MODE A PHRYGIAN $\flat$4 (1 $\flat$2 $\flat$3 $\flat$4 5 $\flat$6 $\flat$7)	iv MODE B$\flat$ LYDIAN $\flat$3 (1 2 $\flat$3 #4 5 6 7)	V MODE C DOMINANT $\flat$2 (1 $\flat$2 3 4 5 6 $\flat$7)	VI MODE D$\flat$ LYDIAN AUG #2 (1 #2 3 #4 5 6 7)	vii MODE E LOCRIAN $\flat\flat$7 (1 $\flat$2 $\flat$3 4 $\flat$5 $\flat$6 $\flat\flat$7)
F	$G°$	$A-$	$B\flat-$	C	$D\flat^+$	$E°$
F^{SUS2}			$B\flat^{SUS2}$			
F^{SUS}				C^{SUS}		
$F^{\flat6}$		$A-^{\flat6}$	$B\flat-^{6}$	C^{6}		
$F^{\triangle}$	$G°$	$A-^{7}$	$B\flat-^{\triangle}$	C^{7}	$D\flat^{\triangle+}$	$E°^{7}$
$F^{\triangle SUS2}$			$B\flat^{\triangle SUS2}$			
$F^{\triangle SUS}$				C^{7SUS}		
				$C^{7/6}$		
			$B\flat-^{9/6}$			
$F^{\triangle 9}$		$A-^{7\flat9}$	$B\flat-^{\triangle 9}$	$C^{\flat9}$		
$F^{\triangle 11}$			$B\flat-^{\triangle #11}$			
			$B\flat-^{\triangle 13#11}$			

I MODE F# HARMONIC MAJ (1 2 3 4 5 b6 7)	ii MODE G# DORIAN b5 (1 2 b3 4 b5 6 b7)	iii MODE A# PHRYGIAN b4 (1 b2 b3 b4 5 b6 b7)	iv MODE B LYDIAN b3 (1 2 b3 #4 5 6 7)	V MODE C# DOMINANT b2 (1 b2 3 4 5 6 b7)	VI MODE D LYDIAN AUG #2 (1 #2 3 #4 #5 6 7)	vii MODE E# LOCRIAN bb7 (1 b2 b3 4 b5 b6 bb7)
$F\#$	$G\#°$	$A\#-$	$B-$	$C\#$	D^+	$E\#°$
$F\#^{SUS2}$			B^{SUS2}			
$F\#^{SUS}$				$C\#^{SUS}$		
$F\#^{b6}$		$A\#-^{b6}$	$B-^6$	$C\#^6$		
$F\#^{\triangle}$	$G\#°$	$A\#-^7$	$B-^{\triangle}$	$C\#^7$	$D^{\triangle+}$	$E\#°^7$
$F\#^{\triangle SUS2}$			$B^{\triangle SUS2}$			
$F\#^{\triangle SUS}$				$C\#^{7SUS}$		
				$C\#^{7/6}$		
			$B-^{9/6}$			
$F\#^{\triangle 9}$		$A\#-^{7b9}$	$B-^{\triangle 9}$	$C\#^{b9}$		
$F\#^{\triangle 11}$			$B-^{\triangle \#11}$			
			$B-^{\triangle 13\#11}$			

THE MATRIX

I MODE G HARMONIC MAJ (1 2 3 4 5 $\flat$6 7)	ii MODE A DORIAN $\flat$5 (1 2 $\flat$3 4 $\flat$5 6 $\flat$7)	iii MODE B PHRYGIAN $\flat$4 (1 $\flat$2 $\flat$3 $\flat$4 5 $\flat$6 $\flat$7)	iv MODE C LYDIAN $\flat$3 (1 2 $\flat$3 #4 5 6 7)	V MODE D DOMINANT $\flat$2 (1 $\flat$2 3 4 5 6 $\flat$7)	VI MODE E$\flat$ LYDIAN AUG #2 (1 #2 3 #4 #5 6 7)	vii MODE F# LOCRIAN $\flat\flat$7 (1 $\flat$2 $\flat$3 4 $\flat$5 $\flat$6 $\flat\flat$7)
G	A$^{\circ}$	B-	C-	D	E$\flat^{+}$	F#$^{\circ}$
G$^{SUS\,2}$			C$^{SUS\,2}$			
G^{SUS}				D^{SUS}		
G$^{\flat6}$		B-$^{\flat6}$	C-^{6}	D^{6}		
G$^{\triangle}$	A$^{\circ}$	B-^{7}	C-$^{\triangle}$	D^{7}	E$\flat^{\triangle+}$	F#$^{\circ7}$
G$^{\triangle\,SUS\,2}$			C$^{\triangle\,SUS\,2}$			
G$^{\triangle\,SUS}$				D$^{7\,SUS}$		
				D$^{7/6}$		
			C-$^{9/6}$			
G$^{\triangle9}$		B-$^{7\flat9}$	C-$^{\triangle9}$	D$^{\flat9}$		
G$^{\triangle11}$			C-$^{\triangle\#11}$			
			C-$^{\triangle13\#11}$			

111

I MODE Ab HARMONIC MAJ (1 2 3 4 5 b6 7)	ii MODE Bb DORIAN b5 (1 2 b3 4 b5 6 b7)	iii MODE C PHRYGIAN b4 (1 b2 b3 b4 5 b6 b7)	iv MODE Db LYDIAN b3 (1 2 b3 #4 5 6 7)	V MODE Eb DOMINANT b2 (1 b2 3 4 5 6 b7)	VI MODE Fb LYDIAN AUG #2 (1 #2 3 #4 #5 6 7)	vii MODE G LOCRIAN bb7 (1 b2 b3 4 b5 b6 bb7)
Ab	Bb°	C⁻	Db⁻	Eb	Fb⁺	G°
Ab SUS 2			Db SUS 2			
Ab SUS				Eb SUS		
Ab b6		C⁻b6	Db⁻6	Eb 6		
Ab △	Bb ⌀	C⁻7	Db⁻△	Eb 7	Fb △+	G°7
Ab △SUS2			Db △SUS2			
Ab △SUS				Eb 7SUS		
				Eb 7/6		
			Db⁻9/6			
Ab △9		C⁻7b9	Db⁻△9	Eb b9		
Ab △11			Db⁻△#11			
			Db⁻△13#11			

THE MATRIX

I MODE A HARMONIC MAJ (1 2 3 4 5 b6 7)	ii MODE B DORIAN b5 (1 2 b3 4 b5 6 b7)	iii MODE C# PHRYGIAN b4 (1 b2 b3 b4 5 b6 b7)	iv MODE D LYDIAN b3 (1 2 b3 #4 5 6 7)	V MODE E DOMINANT b2 (1 b2 3 4 5 6 b7)	VI MODE F LYDIAN AUG #2 (1 #2 3 #4 5 6 7)	vii MODE G# LOCRIAN bb7 (1 b2 b3 4 b5 b6 bb7)
A	B°	$C\#-$	$D-$	E	F^{+}	$G\#^{\circ}$
$A^{SUS\,2}$			$D^{SUS\,2}$			
A^{SUS}				E^{SUS}		
A^{b6}		$C\#-^{b6}$	$D-^{6}$	E^{6}		
$A^{\triangle}$	$B^{\varnothing}$	$C\#-^{7}$	$D-^{\triangle}$	E^{7}	$F^{\triangle+}$	$G\#^{\circ7}$
$A^{\triangle SUS\,2}$			$D^{\triangle SUS\,2}$			
$A^{\triangle SUS}$				$E^{7\,SUS}$		
				$E^{7/6}$		
			$D-^{9/6}$			
$A^{\triangle 9}$		$C\#-^{7b9}$	$D-^{\triangle 9}$	E^{b9}		
$A^{\triangle 11}$			$D-^{\triangle \#11}$			
			$D-^{\triangle 13\#11}$			

THE MATRIX

I MODE Bb HARMONIC MAJ (1 2 3 4 5 b6 7)	ii MODE C DORIAN b5 (1 2 b3 4 b5 6 b7)	iii MODE D PHRYGIAN b4 (1 b2 b3 b4 5 b6 b7)	iv MODE Eb LYDIAN b3 (1 2 b3 #4 5 6 7)	V MODE F DOMINANT b2 (1 b2 3 4 5 6 b7)	VI MODE Gb LYDIAN AUG #2 (1 #2 3 #4 #5 6 7)	vii MODE A LOCRIAN bb7 (1 b2 b3 4 b5 b6 bb7)
Bb	C°	D-	Eb-	F	Gb+	A°
Bb SUS 2			Eb SUS 2			
Bb SUS				F SUS		
Bb b6		D- b6	Eb-- 6	F 6		
Bb △	C°	D- 7	Eb-- △	F 7	Gb △+	A°7
Bb △SUS 2			Eb △SUS 2			
Bb △SUS				F 7 SUS		
				F 7/6		
			Eb- 9/6			
Bb △9		D- 7b9	Eb-- △9	F b9		
Bb △11			Eb- △#11			
			Eb- △13#11			

114

I MODE B HARMONIC MAJ $(1\ 2\ 3\ 4\ 5\ \flat6\ 7)$	ii MODE C# DORIAN $\flat5$ $(1\ 2\ \flat3\ 4\ \flat5\ 6\ \flat7)$	iii MODE D# PHRYGIAN $\flat4$ $(1\ \flat2\ \flat3\ \flat4\ 5\ \flat6\ \flat7)$	iv MODE E LYDIAN $\flat3$ $(1\ 2\ \flat3\ \sharp4\ 5\ 6\ 7)$	V MODE F# DOMINANT $\flat2$ $(1\ \flat2\ 3\ 4\ 5\ 6\ \flat7)$	VI MODE G LYDIAN AUG #2 $(1\ \sharp2\ 3\ \sharp4\ \sharp5\ 6\ 7)$	vii MODE A# LOCRIAN $\flat\flat7$ $(1\ \flat2\ \flat3\ 4\ \flat5\ \flat6\ \flat\flat7)$
B	$C\#°$	$D\#*$	$E\,-$	$F\#$	G^+	$A\#°$
$B^{SUS\,2}$			$E^{SUS\,2}$			
B^{SUS}				$F\#^{SUS}$		
$B^{\flat6}$		$D\#-^{\flat6}$	$E-^{6}$	$F\#^{6}$		
B^{Δ}	$C\#^{ø}$	$D\#-^{7}$	$E-^{\Delta}$	$F\#^{7}$	$G^{\Delta+}$	$A\#°^{7}$
$B^{\Delta SUS\,2}$			$E^{\Delta SUS\,2}$			
$B^{\Delta SUS}$				$F\#^{7\,SUS}$		
				$F\#^{7/6}$		
			$E-^{9/6}$			
$B^{\Delta 9}$		$D\#-^{7\flat9}$	$E-^{\Delta 9}$	$F\#^{\flat9}$		
$B^{\Delta 11}$			$E-^{\Delta \#11}$			
			$E-^{\Delta 13\#11}$			

THE MATRIX

I MODE C HARMONIC MAJ (1 2 3 4 5 b6 7)	ii MODE D DORIAN b5 (1 2 b3 4 b5 6 b7)	iii MODE E PHRYGIAN b4 (1 b2 b3 b4 5 b6 b7)	iv MODE F LYDIAN b3 (1 2 b3 #4 5 6 7)	V MODE G DOMINANT b2 (1 b2 3 4 5 6 b7)	VI MODE Ab LYDIAN AUG #2 (1 #2 3 #4 5 6 7)	vii MODE B LOCRIAN bb7 (1 b2 b3 4 b5 b6 bb7)
C	D°	E^{-}	F^{-}	G	Ab^{+}	B°
$C^{SUS\,2}$			$F^{SUS\,2}$			
C^{SUS}				G^{SUS}		
C^{b6}		E^{-b6}	F^{-6}	G^{6}		
$C^{\triangle}$	$D^{\emptyset}$	E^{-7}	$F^{-\triangle}$	G^{7}	$Ab^{\triangle+}$	$B^{\circ7}$
$C^{\triangle SUS\,2}$			$F^{\triangle SUS\,2}$			
$C^{\triangle SUS}$				$G^{7\,SUS}$		
				$G^{7/6}$		
			$F^{-9/6}$			
$C^{\triangle 9}$		E^{-7b9}	$F^{-\triangle 9}$	G^{b9}		
$C^{\triangle 11}$			$F^{-\triangle\#11}$			
			$F^{-\triangle 13\#11}$			

116

THE MATRIX

I MODE C# HARMONIC MAJ (1 2 3 4 5 b6 7)	ii MODE D# DORIAN b5 (1 2 b3 4 b5 6 b7)	iii MODE E# PHRYGIAN b4 (1 b2 b3 b4 5 b6 b7)	iv MODE F# LYDIAN b3 (1 2 b3 #4 5 6 7)	V MODE G# DOMINANT b2 (1 b2 3 4 5 6 b7)	VI MODE A LYDIAN AUG #2 (1 #2 3 #4 #5 6 7)	vii MODE B# LOCRIAN bb7 (1 b2 b3 4 b5 b6 bb7)
$C\#$	$D\#^{\circ}$	$E\#{-}$	$F\#{-}$	$G\#$	A^{+}	$B\#^{\circ}$
$C\#^{SUS\,2}$			$F\#^{SUS\,2}$			
$C\#^{SUS}$				$G\#^{SUS}$		
$C\#^{b6}$		$E\#{-}^{b6}$	$F\#{-}^{6}$	$G\#^{6}$		
$C\#^{\triangle}$	$D\#^{\circ}$	$E\#{-}^{7}$	$F\#{-}^{\triangle}$	$G\#^{7}$	$A^{\triangle+}$	$B\#^{\circ 7}$
$C\#^{\triangle SUS\,2}$			$F\#^{\triangle SUS\,2}$			
$C\#^{\triangle SUS}$				$G\#^{7\,SUS}$		
				$G\#^{7/6}$		
			$F\#{-}^{9/6}$			
$C\#^{\triangle 9}$		$E\#{-}^{7\,b9}$	$F\#{-}^{\triangle 9}$	$G\#^{b9}$		
$C\#^{\triangle 11}$			$F\#{-}^{\triangle \#11}$			
			$F\#{-}^{\triangle 13\#11}$			

THE MATRIX

I MODE	ii MODE	iii MODE	iv MODE	V MODE	VI MODE	vii MODE
D HARMONIC MAJ (1 2 3 4 5 b6 7)	E DORIAN b5 (1 2 b3 4 b5 6 b7)	F# PHRYGIAN b4 (1 b2 b3 b4 5 b6 b7)	G LYDIAN b3 (1 2 b3 #4 5 6 7)	A DOMINANT b2 (1 b2 3 4 5 6 b7)	Bb LYDIAN AUG #2 (1 #2 3 #4 5 6 7)	C# LOCRIAN bb7 (1 b2 b3 4 b5 b6 bb7)
D	E°	$F\#\text{-}$	$G\text{-}$	A	$B\flat^{+}$	$C\#^{\circ}$
$D^{sus\,2}$			$G^{sus\,2}$			
D^{sus}				A^{sus}		
$D^{\flat6}$		$F\#\text{-}^{\flat6}$	$G\text{-}^{6}$	A^{6}		
$D^{\triangle}$	$E^{\#}$	$F\#\text{-}^{7}$	$G\text{-}^{\triangle}$	A^{7}	$B\flat^{\triangle+}$	$C\#^{\circ7}$
$D^{\triangle sus\,2}$			$G^{\triangle sus\,2}$			
$D^{\triangle sus}$				$A^{7\,sus}$		
				$A^{7/6}$		
			$G\text{-}^{9/6}$			
$D^{\triangle 9}$		$F\#\text{-}^{7\flat9}$	$G\text{-}^{\triangle 9}$	$A^{\flat9}$		
$D^{\triangle 11}$			$G\text{-}^{\triangle \#11}$			
			$G\text{-}^{\triangle 13\#11}$			

I MODE Eb HARMONIC MAJ (1 2 3 4 5 b6 7)	ii MODE F DORIAN b5 (1 2 b3 4 b5 6 b7)	iii MODE G PHRYGIAN b4 (1 b2 b3 b4 5 b6 b7)	iv MODE Ab LYDIAN b3 (1 2 b3 #4 5 6 7)	V MODE Bb DOMINANT b2 (1 b2 3 4 5 6 b7)	VI MODE Cb LYDIAN AUG #2 (1 #2 3 #4 #5 6 7)	vii MODE D LOCRIAN bb7 (1 b2 b3 4 b5 b6 bb7)
Eb	$F°$	$G-$	$Ab-$	Bb	Cb^+	$D°$
$Eb^{SUS\,2}$			$Ab^{SUS\,2}$			
Eb^{SUS}				Bb^{SUS}		
Eb^{b6}		$G-^{b6}$	$Ab-^{6}$	Bb^{6}		
$Eb^{\triangle}$	$F^{\#}$	$G-^{7}$	$Ab-^{\triangle}$	Bb^{7}	$Cb^{\triangle+}$	$D°^{7}$
$Eb^{\triangle SUS\,2}$			$Ab^{\triangle SUS\,2}$			
$Eb^{\triangle SUS}$				$Bb^{7\,SUS}$		
				$Bb'^{7/6}$		
			$Ab^{9/6}$			
$Eb^{\triangle 9}$		$G-^{7b9}$	$Ab-^{\triangle 9}$	Bb^{b9}		
$Eb^{\triangle 11}$			$Ab-^{\triangle \#11}$			
			$Ab-^{\triangle 13\#11}$			

THE MATRIX

I MODE E HARMONIC MAJ (1 2 3 4 5 b6 7)	ii MODE F# DORIAN b5 (1 2 b3 4 b5 6 b7)	iii MODE G# PHRYGIAN b4 (1 b2 b3 b4 5 b6 b7)	iv MODE A LYDIAN b3 (1 2 b3 #4 5 6 7)	V MODE B DOMINANT b2 (1 b2 3 4 5 6 b7)	VI MODE C LYDIAN AUG #2 (1 #2 3 #4 5 6 7)	vii MODE D# LOCRIAN bb7 (1 b2 b3 4 b5 b6 bb7)
E	$F\#^{\circ}$	$G\#-$	$A-$	B	C^{+}	$D\#^{\circ}$
$E^{SUS\,2}$			$A^{SUS\,2}$			
E^{SUS}				B^{SUS}		
E^{b6}		$G\#-^{b6}$	$A-^{6}$	B^{6}		
$E^{\triangle}$	$F\#^{\#^{\circ}}$	$G\#-^{7}$	$A-^{\triangle}$	B^{7}	$C^{\triangle+}$	$D\#^{\circ\,7}$
$E^{\triangle SUS\,2}$			$A^{\triangle SUS\,2}$			
$E^{\triangle SUS}$				$B^{7\,SUS}$		
				$B^{7/6}$		
			$A-^{9/6}$			
$E^{\triangle 9}$		$G\#-^{7b9}$	$A-^{\triangle 9}$	B^{b9}		
$E^{\triangle 11}$			$A-^{\triangle\#11}$			
			$A-^{\triangle 13\#11}$			

THE IONIAN FLAT FIVE SCALE

I MODE - F IONIAN FLAT FIVE

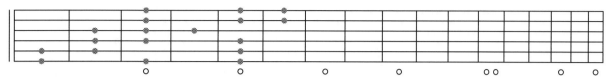

BASIC TRIAD - F FLAT FIVE (1 3 ♭5)

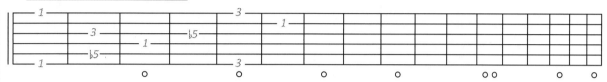

F MAJOR SEVENTH FLAT FIVE (1 3 ♭5 7)

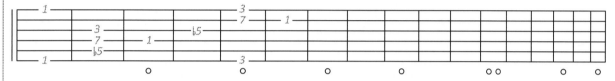

ARPEGGIO OPTIONS

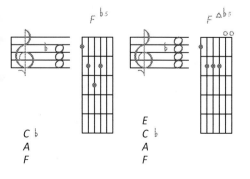

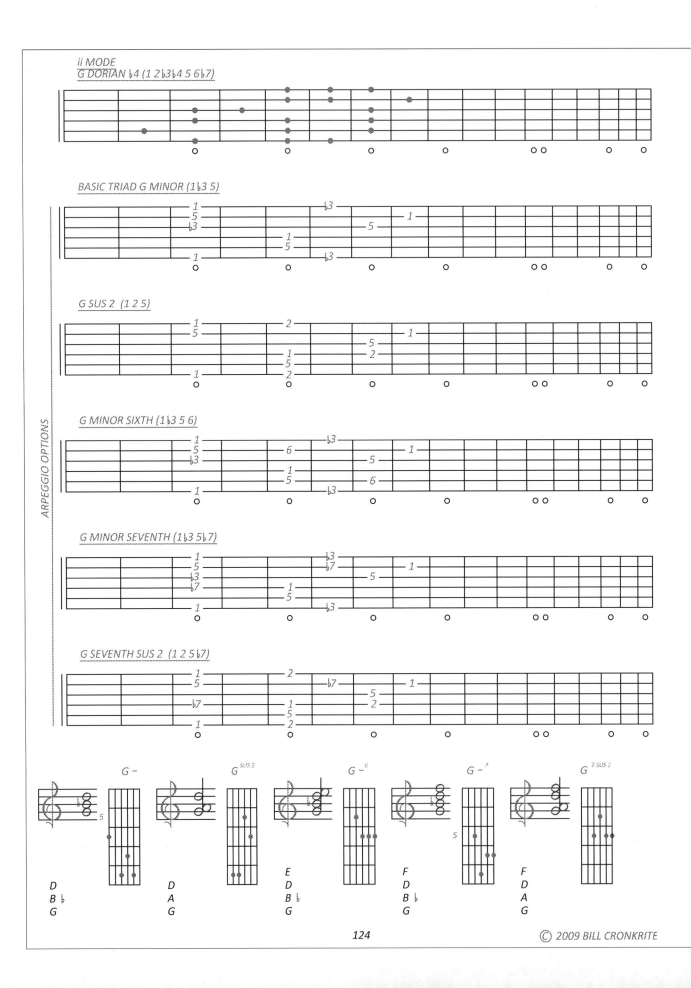

ii MODE
G DORIAN ♭4 (1 2 ♭3 ♭4 5 6 ♭7)

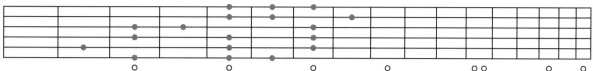

G MINOR NINE/SIX (1 ♭3 5 6 9)

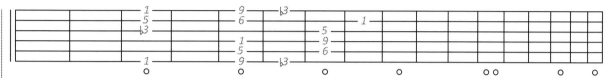

G MINOR NINTH (1 ♭3 5 ♭7 9)

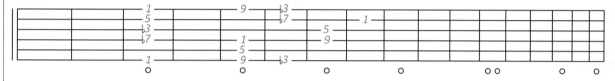

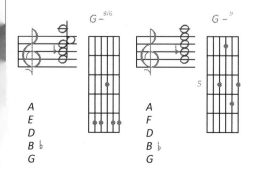

iii MODE
A PHRYGIAN ♮3 (1 ♭2 ♮3 4 5 ♭6 ♭7)

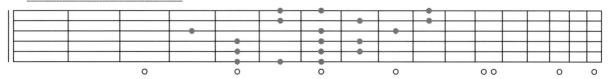

A SUS (1 4 5)

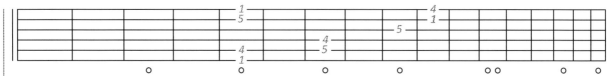

A SEVENTH SUS (1 4 5 ♭7)

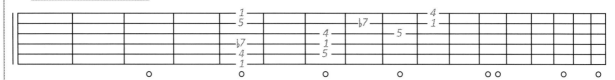

ARPEGGIO OPTIONS

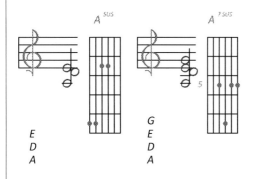

126

IV MODE
B♭ LYDIAN ♭2 (1 ♭2 3♯4 5 6 7)

BASIC TRIAD (1 3 5)

B♭ SIXTH (1 3 5 6)

B♭ MAJOR SEVENTH (1 3 5 7)

B♭ MAJOR SEVENTH FLAT NINE (1 3 5 7♭9)

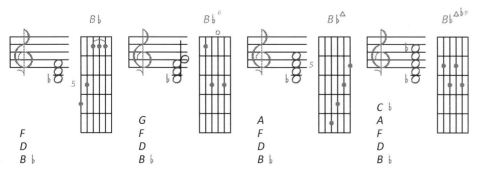

B♭

B♭⁶

B♭△

B♭△♭⁹

F
D
B♭

G
F
D
B♭

A
F
D
B♭

C♭
A
F
D
B♭

127

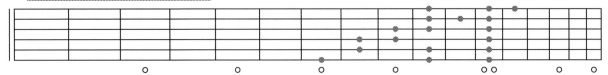

V MODE
C♭ *SUPERLYDIAN AUG (1 2♯3♯4♯5♯6♯7)*

<u>*THIS MODE HAS NO TRADITIONAL CHORD FORMS*</u>

Certainly there are chords that can be constructed to harmonize with this scale but the presence of the sharp in the third negates any traditional chord spellings or voicings.

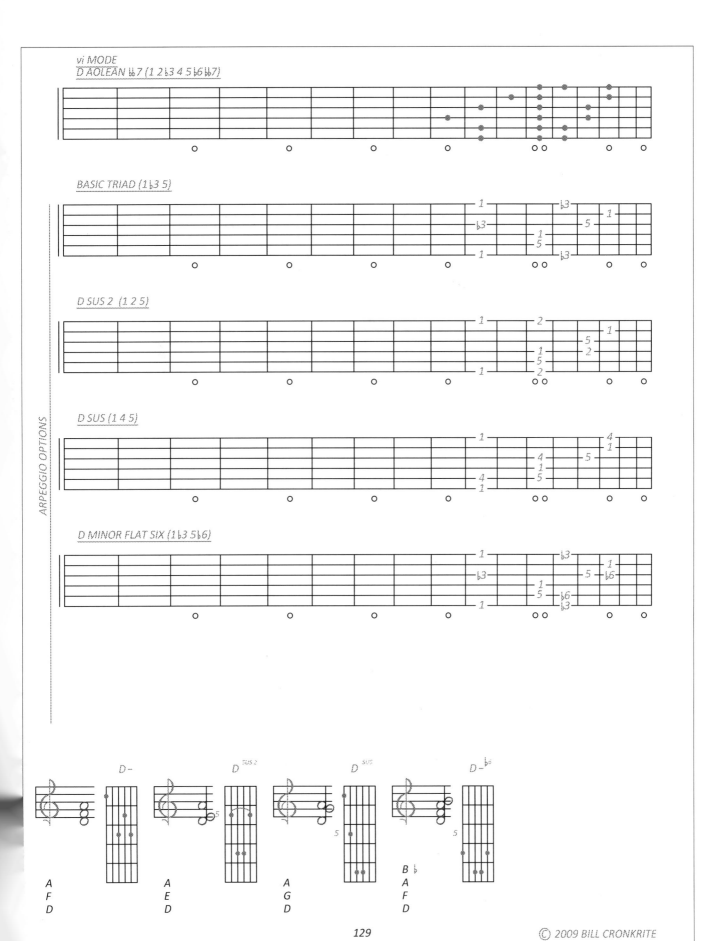

vii MODE
E LOCRIAN ♭♭6 (1 ♭2 ♭3 4 ♭5 ♭♭6 ♭7)

BASIC TRIAD (1 ♭3 ♭5)

E HALF DIMINISHED SEVENTH (1 ♭3 ♭5 ♭7)

ARPEGGIO OPTIONS

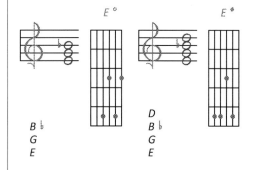

I MODE F IONIAN ♭5 (1 2 3 4 ♭5 6 7)	ii MODE G DORIAN ♭4 (1 2 ♭3 ♭4 5 6 ♭7)	iii MODE A PHRYGIAN ♭♭3 (1 ♭2 ♭♭3 4 5 ♭6 ♭7)	IV MODE B♭ LYDIAN ♭2 (1 ♭2 3 #4 5 6 7)	V MODE C♭ SUPERLYDIAN AUG (1 #2 #3 #4 #5 #6 7)	vi MODE D AOLEAN ♭♭7 (1 2 ♭3 4 5 ♭6 ♭♭7)	vii MODE E LOCRIAN ♭♭6 (1 ♭2 ♭3 4 ♭5 ♭♭6 ♭7)
F♭5	G-		B♭		D-	E°
	G sus2				D sus2	
		A sus			D sus	
	G-6		B♭6		D-♭6	
F△♭5	G-7		B♭△			E*
	G 7sus2					
		A 7sus				
	G-9/6					
	G-9		B♭△♭9			

I MODE F# IONIAN b5 (1 2 3 4 b5 6 7)	ii MODE G# DORIAN b4 (1 2 b3 b4 5 6 b7)	iii MODE A# PHRYGIAN bb3 (1 b2 bb3 4 5 b6 b7)	IV MODE B LYDIAN b2 (1 b2 3 #4 5 6 7)	V MODE C SUPERLYDIAN AUG (1 #2 #3 #4 #5 #6 7)	vi MODE D# AOLEAN bb7 (1 2 b3 4 5 b6 bb7)	vii MODE E LOCRIAN bb6 (1 b2 b3 4 b5 bb6 b7)
F#^{b5}	G#-		B		D#-	E#°
	G#$^{SUS\,2}$				D#$^{SUS\,2}$	
		A#^{SUS}			D#^{SUS}	
	G#-^{6}		B^{6}		D#-^{b6}	
F#$^{\Delta b5}$	G#-^{7}		B$^{\Delta}$			E#^{ø}
	G#$^{7\,SUS\,2}$					
		A#$^{7\,SUS}$				
	G#-$^{9/6}$					
	G#-^{9}		B$_{\Delta}$b^{9}			

I MODE G IONIAN b5 (1 2 3 4 b5 6 7)	ii MODE A DORIAN b4 (1 2 b3 b4 5 6 b7)	iii MODE B PHRYGIAN bb3 (1 b2 bb3 4 5 b6 b7)	IV MODE C LYDIAN b2 (1 b2 3 #4 5 6 7)	V MODE Db SUPERLYDIAN AUG (1 #2 #3 #4 #5 #6 7)	vi MODE E AOLEAN bb7 (1 2 b3 4 5 b6 bb7)	vii MODE F# LOCRIAN bb6 (1 b2 b3 4 b5 bb6 b7)
G^{b5}	A^-		C		E^-	$F\#°$
	$A^{SUS\,2}$				$E^{SUS\,2}$	
		B^{SUS}			E^{SUS}	
	$A^{-\,6}$		C^6		$E^{-\,b6}$	
$G^{\triangle b5}$	$A^{-\,7}$		$C^{\triangle}$			$F\#^{\#}$
	$A^{7\,SUS\,2}$					
		$B^{7\,SUS}$				
	$A^{-\,9/6}$					
	$A^{-\,9}$		$C^{\triangle b\,9}$			

I MODE Ab IONIAN b5 (1 2 3 4b 5 6 7)	ii MODE Bb DORIAN b4 (1 2 b3 b4 5 6 b7)	iii MODE C PHRYGIAN bb3 (1 b2 bb3 4 5 b6 b7)	IV MODE Db LYDIAN b2 (1 b2 3 #4 5 6 7)	V MODE Eb SUPERLYDIAN AUG (1 #2 #3 #4 #5 #6 7)	vi MODE F AOLEAN bb7 (1 2 b3 4 5 b6 bb7)	vii MODE G LOCRIAN bb6 (1 b2 b3 4 b5 bb6 b7)
Ab^{b5}	$Bb-$		Db		$F-$	G°
	$Bb^{SUS\,2}$				$F^{SUS\,2}$	
		C^{SUS}			F^{SUS}	
	$Bb-^{6}$		Db^{6}		$F-^{b6}$	
$Ab^{\Delta b5}$	$Bb-^{7}$		Db^{Δ}			G^{*}
	$Bb^{7\,SUS\,2}$					
		$C^{7\,SUS}$				
	$Bb-^{9/6}$					
	$Bb-^{9}$		$Db^{\Delta b\,9}$			

I MODE A IONIAN ♭5 (1 2 3 ♭5 6 7)	ii MODE B DORIAN ♭4 (1 2 ♭3 ♭4 5 6 ♭7)	iii MODE C# PHRYGIAN ♭♭3 (1 ♭2 ♭♭3 4 5 ♭6 ♭7)	IV MODE D LYDIAN ♭2 (1 ♭2 3 4 #5 6 7)	V MODE E♭ SUPERLYDIAN AUG (1 #2 #3 #4 #5 #6 7)	vi MODE F# AOLEAN ♭♭7 (1 2 ♭3 4 5 ♭6 ♭♭7)	vii MODE G# LOCRIAN ♭♭6 (1 ♭2 ♭3 4 ♭5 ♭♭6 ♭7)
$A^{\flat 5}$	$B\text{--}$		D		$F\#\text{--}$	$G\#^{\circ}$
	$B^{SUS\,2}$				$F\#^{SUS\,2}$	
		$C\#^{SUS}$			$F\#^{SUS}$	
	$B\text{--}^{6}$		D^{6}		$F\#\text{--}^{\flat 6}$	
$A^{\triangle\flat 5}$	$B\text{--}^{7}$		$D^{\triangle}$			$G\#^{\#}$
	$B^{7\,SUS\,2}$					
		$C\#^{7\,SUS}$				
	$B\text{--}^{9/6}$					
	$B\text{--}^{9}$		$D^{\triangle\flat 9}$			

I MODE Bb IONIAN b5 (1 2 3 4 b5 6 7)	ii MODE C DORIAN b4 (1 2 b3 b4 5 6 b7)	iii MODE D PHRYGIAN bb3 (1 b2 bb3 4 5 b6 b7)	IV MODE Eb LYDIAN b2 (1 b2 3 #4 5 6 7)	V MODE Fb SUPERLYDIAN AUG (1 #2 #3 #4 #5 #6 7)	vi MODE G AOLEAN bb7 (1 2 3 4 5 b6 bb7)	vii MODE A LOCRIAN bb6 (1 b2 b3 4 b5 bb6 b7)
Bb^{b5}	C^{-}		Eb		G^{-}	A°
	$C^{SUS\,2}$				$G^{SUS\,2}$	
		D^{SUS}			G^{SUS}	
	C^{-6}		Eb^{6}		G^{-b6}	
$Bb^{\Delta b5}$	C^{-7}		Eb^{Δ}			$A^{\bullet}$
	$C^{7\,SUS\,2}$					
		$D^{7\,SUS}$				
	$C^{-9/6}$					
	C^{-9}		$Eb^{\Delta b9}$			

I MODE B IONIAN ♭5 (1 2 3 4 ♭5 6 7)	ii MODE C# DORIAN ♭4 (1 2 ♭3 ♭4 5 6 ♭7)	iii MODE D# PHRYGIAN ♭♭3 (1 ♭2 ♭♭3 4 5 ♭6 ♭7)	IV MODE E LYDIAN ♭2 (1 ♭2 3 #4 5 6 7)	V MODE F SUPERLYDIAN AUG (1 #2 #3 #4 #5 #6 7)	vi MODE G# AOLEAN ♭♭7 (1 2 ♭3 4 5 ♭6 ♭♭7)	vii MODE A# LOCRIAN ♭♭6 (1 ♭2 ♭3 4 ♭5 ♭♭6 ♭7)
$B^{\flat 5}$	$C\sharp{-}$		E		$G\sharp{-}$	$A\sharp^{\circ}$
	$C\sharp^{SUS\,2}$				$G\sharp^{SUS\,2}$	
		$D\sharp^{SUS}$			$G\sharp^{SUS}$	
	$C\sharp{-}^{6}$		E^{6}		$G\sharp{-}^{\flat 5}$	
$B^{\triangle\flat 5}$	$C\sharp{-}^{7}$		$E^{\triangle}$			$A\sharp^{\varnothing}$
	$C\sharp^{7\,SUS\,2}$					
		$D\sharp^{7\,SUS}$				
	$C\sharp{-}^{9/6}$					
	$C\sharp{-}^{9}$		$E^{\triangle\flat 9}$			

I MODE C IONIAN ♭5 (1 2 3 4 ♭5 6 7)	ii MODE D DORIAN ♭4 (1 2 ♭3 ♭4 5 6 ♭7)	iii MODE E PHRYGIAN ♭♭3 (1 ♭2 ♭♭3 4 5 ♭6 ♭7)	IV MODE F LYDIAN ♭2 (1 ♭2 3 #4 5 6 7)	V MODE G♭ SUPERLYDIAN AUG (1 #2 #3 #4 #5 #6 7)	vi MODE A AOLEAN ♭♭7 (1 2 ♭3 4 5 ♭6 ♭♭7)	vii MODE B LOCRIAN ♭♭6 (1 ♭2 ♭3 4 ♭5 ♭♭6 ♭7)
$C^{\flat5}$	D^{-}		F		A^{-}	B°
	$D^{SUS\,2}$				$A^{SUS\,2}$	
		E^{SUS}			A^{SUS}	
	$D^{-\,6}$		F^{6}		$A^{-\,\flat5}$	
$C^{\Delta\flat5}$	$D^{-\,7}$		F^{Δ}			B^{*}
	$D^{7\,SUS\,2}$					
		$E^{7\,SUS}$				
	$D^{-\,9/6}$					
	$D^{-\,9}$		$F^{\Delta\flat9}$			

I MODE Db IONIAN b5 (1 2 3 4 b5 6 7)	ii MODE Eb DORIAN b4 (1 2 b3 b4 5 6 b7)	iii MODE F PHRYGIAN bb3 (1 b2 bb3 4 5 b6 b7)	IV MODE Gb LYDIAN b2 (1 b2 3 #4 5 6 7)	V MODE Abb SUPERLYDIAN AUG (1 #2 #3 #4 #5 #6 7)	vi MODE Bb AOLEAN bb7 (1 2 b3 4 5 b6 bb7)	vii MODE C LOCRIAN bb6 (1 b2 b3 4 b5 bb6 b7)
Db b5	Eb−		Gb		Bb−	C°
	Eb SUS 2				Bb SUS 2	
		F SUS			Bb SUS	
	Eb−6		Gb6		Bb− b6	
Db Δb5	Eb−7		Gb Δ			C *
	Eb 7 SUS 2					
		F 7 SUS				
	Eb−9/6					
	Eb−9		Gb Δb9			

139

I MODE D IONIAN b5 (1 2 3 4 b5 6 7)	ii MODE E DORIAN b4 (1 2 b3 b4 5 6 b7)	iii MODE F# PHRYGIAN bb3 (1 b2 bb3 4 5 b6 b7)	IV MODE G LYDIAN b2 (1 b2 3 #4 5 6 7)	V MODE Ab SUPERLYDIAN AUG (1 #2 #3 #4 #5 #6 7)	vi MODE B AOLEAN bb7 (1 2 b3 4 5 b6 bb7)	vii MODE C# LOCRIAN bb6 (1 b2 b3 4 b5 bb6 b7)
D^{b5}	E^{-}		G		B^{-}	$C\#°$
	$E^{SUS\,2}$				$B^{SUS\,2}$	
		$F\#^{SUS}$			B^{SUS}	
	E^{-6}		G^{6}		B^{-b6}	
$D^{\triangle b5}$	E^{-7}		$G^{\triangle}$			$C\#^{ø}$
	$E^{7\,SUS\,2}$					
		$F\#^{7\,SUS}$				
	$E^{-9/6}$					
	E^{-9}		$G^{\triangle b9}$			

I MODE Eb IONIAN b5 (1 2 3 4 b5 6 7)	ii MODE F DORIAN b4 (1 2 b3 b4 5 6 b7)	iii MODE G PHRYGIAN bb3 (1 b2 bb3 4 5 b6 b7)	IV MODE Ab LYDIAN b2 (1 b2 3 #4 5 6 7)	V MODE Bbb SUPERLYDIAN AUG (1 #2 #3 #4 #5 #6 7)	vi MODE C AOLEAN bb7 (1 2 b3 4 5 b6 bb7)	vii MODE D LOCRIAN bb6 (1 b2 b3 4 b5 bb6 b7)
Eb b5	F -		Ab		C -	D °
	F sus2				C sus2	
		G sus			C sus	
	F - 6		Ab 6		C - b5	
Eb Δb5	F - 7		Ab Δ			D ø
	F 7 sus2					
		G 7 sus				
	F - 9/6					
	F - 9		Ab Δb9			

I MODE E IONIAN b5 (1 2 3 4 b5 6 7)	ii MODE F# DORIAN b4 (1 2 b3 b4 5 6 b7)	iii MODE G# PHRYGIAN bb3 (1 b2 bb3 4 5 b6 b7)	IV MODE A LYDIAN b2 (1 b2 3 #4 5 6 7)	V MODE Bb SUPERLYDIAN AUG (1 #2 #3 #4 #5 #6 7)	vi MODE C# AOLEAN bb7 (1 2 b3 4 5 b6 bb7)	vii MODE D# LOCRIAN bb6 (1 b2 b3 4 b5 bb6 b7)
E^{b5}	$F\#-$		A		$C\#-$	$D\#°$
	$F\#^{SUS\,2}$				$C\#^{SUS\,2}$	
		$G\#^{SUS}$			$C\#^{SUS}$	
	$F\#-^{6}$		A^{6}		$C\#-^{b6}$	
$E^{\triangle b5}$	$F\#-^{7}$		$A^{\triangle}$			$D\#^{ø}$
	$F\#^{7\,SUS\,2}$					
		$G\#^{7\,SUS}$				
	$F\#-^{9/6}$					
	$F\#-^{9}$		$A^{\triangle b9}$			

THE HUNGARIAN MINOR

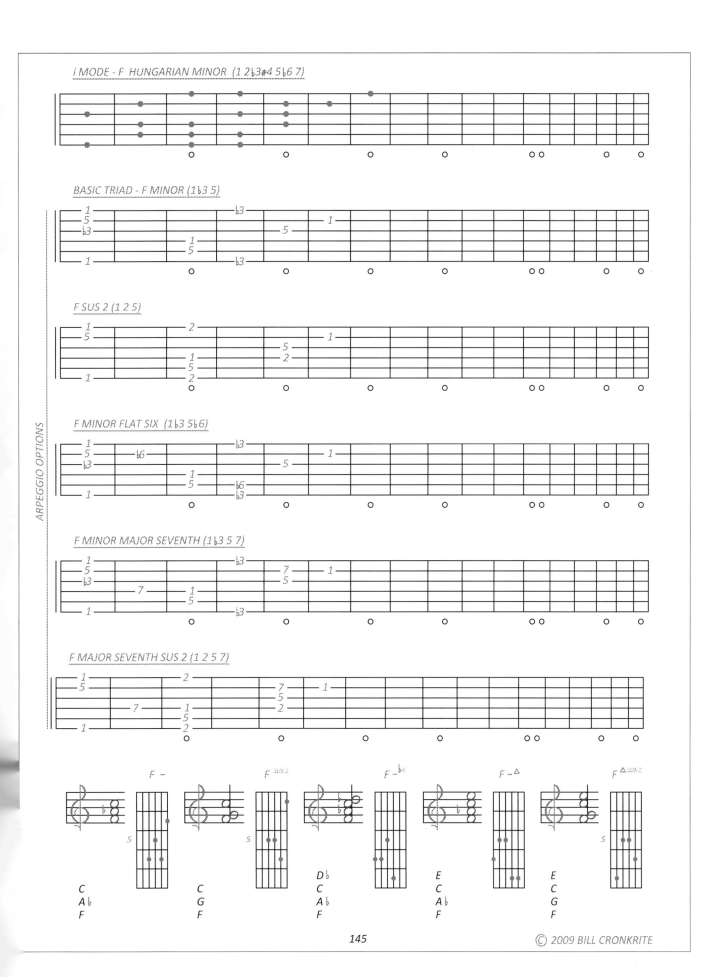

i MODE - F HUNGARIAN MINOR (1 2 ♭3 #4 5 ♭6 7)

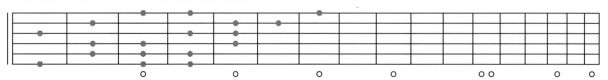

F MINOR MAJOR NINTH (1 ♭3 5 7 9)

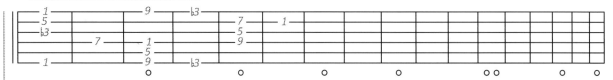

F MINOR MAJOR ELEVENTH (1 ♭3 5 7 9 #11)

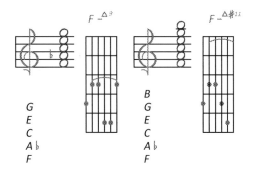

146

II MODE
G ORIENTAL (1♭2 3 4♭5 6♭7)

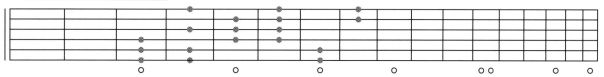

BASIC TRIAD G FLAT FIVE (1 3♭5)

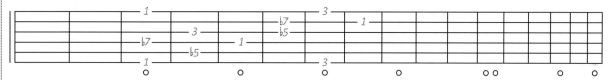

G SEVENTH FLAT FIVE (1 3♭5♭7)

G SEVENTH FLAT FIVE FLAT NINE (1 3♭5♭7♭9)

ARPEGGIO OPTIONS

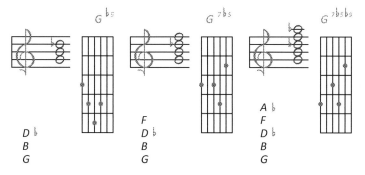

$G^{♭5}$ $G^{7♭5}$ $G^{7♭5♭9}$

D♭   F♭   A♭
B   D♭   F
G   B   D♭
         G   B
                  G

147

III MODE
Ab IONIAN   AUG#2 (1 #2 3 4 #5 6 7)

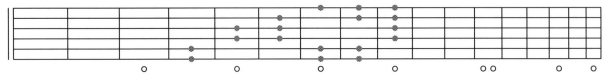

BASIC TRIAD Ab AUGMENTED (1 3 #5)

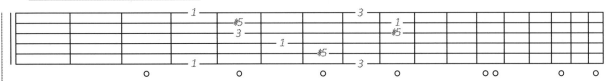

Ab MAJOR SEVENTH AUGMENTED (1 3 #5 7)

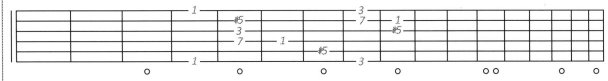

ARPEGGIO OPTIONS

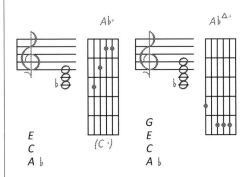

iv MODE
B LOCRIAN ♭♭3 ♭♭7 (1 2 ♭♭3 4 5 6 ♭♭7)

THIS MODE HAS NO TRADITIONAL CHORD FORMS

Certainly there are chords that can be constructed to harmonize with this scale but the presence of the double flat in the third negates any traditional chord spellings or voicings.

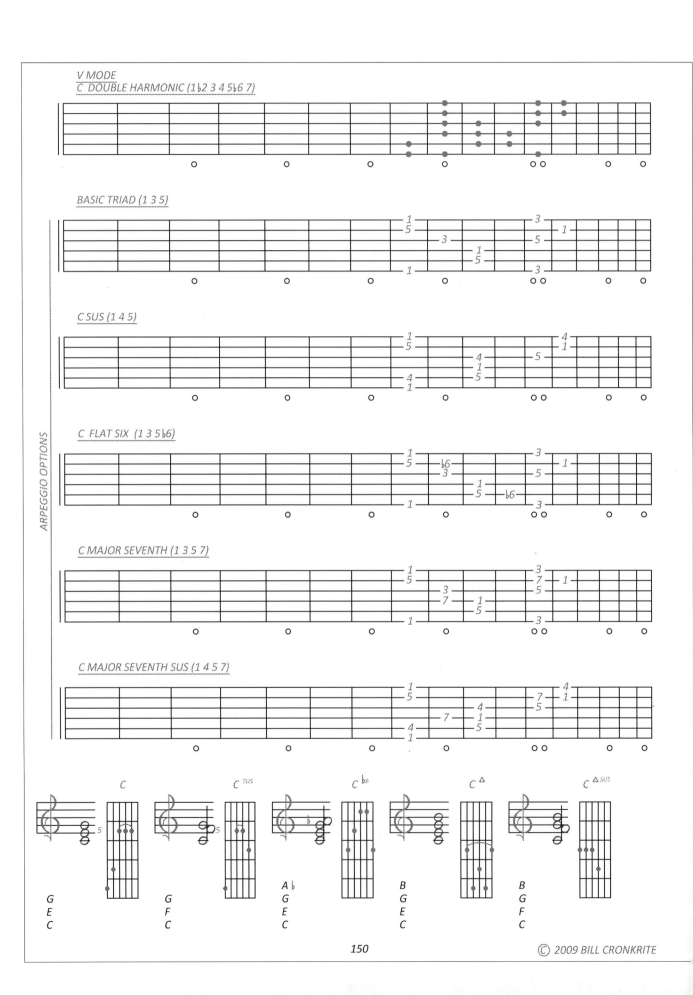

<u>V MODE</u>
<u>C DOUBLE HARMONIC (1♭2 3 4 5♭6 7)</u>

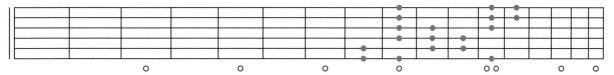

<u>C MAJOR SEVENTH FLAT NINE (1 3 5 7♭9)</u>

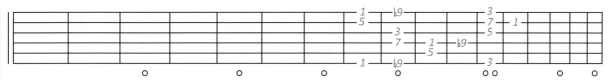

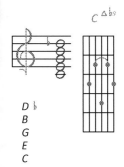

$C^{\triangle\,♭9}$

D♭
B
G
E
C

VI MODE
D♭ LYDIAN #6#2 (1#2 3#4 5#6 7)

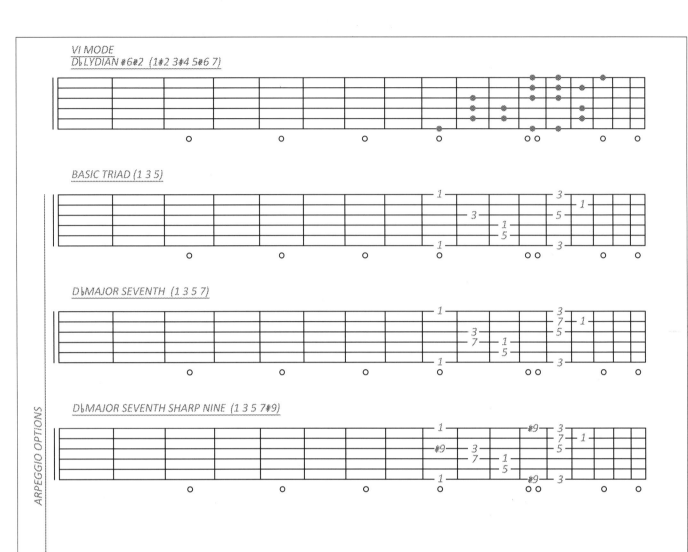

BASIC TRIAD (1 3 5)

D♭ MAJOR SEVENTH (1 3 5 7)

D♭ MAJOR SEVENTH SHARP NINE (1 3 5 7#9)

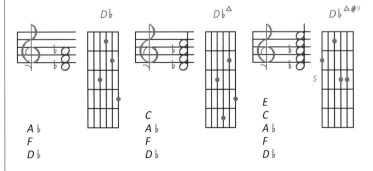

D♭

A♭
F
D♭

D♭△

C
A♭
F
D♭

D♭△#9

E
C
A♭
F
D♭

152

vii MODE
(1♭2♭3♭4 5♭6♭♭7)

BASIC TRIAD (1♭3 5)

E MINOR FLAT SIX (1♭3 5♭6)

ARPEGGIO OPTIONS

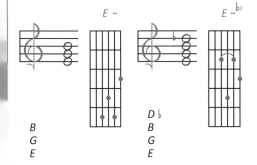

E --

E --♭6

B
G
E

D♭
B
G
E

i MODE F HUNGARIAN MIN (1 2 b3 #4 5 b6 7)	ii MODE G ORIENTAL (1 b2 3 4 b5 6 b7)	iii MODE Ab IONIAN AUG #2 (1 #2 3 4 #5 6 7)	iv MODE B LOCRIAN bb3 bb7 (1 b2 bb3 4 b5 b6 bb7)	V MODE C DOUBLE HARMONIC (1 b2 3 4 5 b6 7)	VI MODE Db LYDIAN #6 #2 (1 #2 3 #4 5 #6 7)	vii MODE (1 b2 b3 b4 5 b6 bb7)
$F-$	G^{b5}	Ab^{+}		C	Db	$E-$
F^{SUS2}						
				C^{SUS}		
$F-^{b6}$				C^{b6}		$E-^{b6}$
$F-^{\triangle}$	G^{7b5}	$Ab^{\triangle+}$		$C^{\triangle}$	$Db^{\triangle}$	
$F^{\triangle SUS2}$						
				$C^{\triangle SUS}$		
$F-^{\triangle 9}$	G^{7b5b9}			$C^{\triangle b9}$	$Db^{\triangle \#9}$	
$F-^{\triangle \#11}$						

154

i MODE F# HUNGARIAN MIN ($1\ 2\ b3\ \#4\ 5\ b6\ 7$)	II MODE G# ORIENTAL ($1\ b2\ 3\ 4\ b5\ 6\ b7$)	III MODE A IONIAN AUG #2 ($1\ \#2\ 3\ 4\ \#5\ 6\ 7$)	iv MODE B# LOCRIAN bb3 bb7 ($1\ b2\ bb3\ 4\ b5\ b6\ bb7$)	V MODE C# DOUBLE HARMONIC ($1\ b2\ 3\ 4\ 5\ b6\ 7$)	VI MODE D LYDIAN #6 #2 ($1\ \#2\ 3\ \#4\ 5\ \#6\ 7$)	vii MODE ($1\ b2\ b3\ b4\ 5\ b6\ bb7$)
F#-	G#^{b5}	A^{+}		C#	D	E#-
F#$^{SUS\,2}$						
				C#^{SUS}		
F#-^{b6}				C#^{b5}		E#-^{b6}
F#-$^{\triangle}$	G#^{7b5}	A$^{\triangle+}$		C#$^{\triangle}$	D$^{\triangle}$	
F#$^{\triangle SUS\,2}$						
				C#$^{\triangle SUS}$		
F#-$^{\triangle 9}$	G#^{7b5b9}			C#$^{\triangle b9}$	D$^{\triangle \#9}$	
F#-$^{\triangle \#11}$						

i MODE G HUNGARIAN MIN $(1\ 2\ \flat3\ \sharp4\ 5\ \flat6\ 7)$	II MODE A ORIENTAL $(1\ \flat2\ 3\ 4\ \flat5\ \flat6\ \flat7)$	III MODE B$\flat$ IONIAN AUG #2 $(1\ \sharp2\ 3\ 4\ \sharp5\ 6\ 7)$	iv MODE C# LOCRIAN $\flat\flat3\ \flat\flat7$ $(1\ \flat2\ \flat\flat3\ 4\ \flat5\ \flat6\ \flat\flat7)$	V MODE D DOUBLE HARMONIC $(1\ \flat2\ 3\ 4\ 5\ \flat6\ 7)$	VI MODE E$\flat$ LYDIAN #6 #2 $(1\ \sharp2\ 3\ \sharp4\ 5\ \sharp6\ 7)$	vii MODE $(1\ \flat2\ \flat3\ \flat4\ 5\ \flat6\ \flat\flat7)$
G^-	$A^{\flat5}$	$B\flat^+$		D	$E\flat$	$F\sharp^-$
$G^{sus\,2}$						
				D^{sus}		
$G^{-\flat6}$				$D^{\flat6}$		$F\sharp^{-\flat6}$
$G^{-\triangle}$	$A^{7\flat5}$	$B\flat^{\triangle+}$		$D^{\triangle}$	$E\flat^{\triangle}$	
$G^{\triangle sus\,2}$						
				$D^{\triangle sus}$		
$G^{-\triangle 9}$	$A^{7\flat5\flat9}$			$D^{\triangle\flat9}$	$E\flat^{\triangle\sharp9}$	
$G^{-\triangle\sharp11}$						

156

i MODE Ab HUNGARIAN MIN (1 2 b3 #4 5 b6 7)	II MODE Bb ORIENTAL (1 b2 3 4 b5 6 b7)	III MODE Cb IONIAN AUG #2 (1 #2 3 4 #5 6 7)	iv MODE D LOCRIAN bb3 bb7 (1 b2 bb3 4 b5 b6 bb7)	V MODE Eb DOUBLE HARMONIC (1 b2 3 4 5 b6 7)	VI MODE Fb LYDIAN #6 #2 (1 #2 #4 5 #6 7)	vii MODE (1 b2 b3 b4 5 b6 bb7)
Ab-	Bb b5	Cb +		Eb	Fb	G-
Ab sus2						
				Eb sus		
Ab- b6				Eb b6		G- b6
Ab-△	Bb 7b5	Cb△+		Eb△	Fb△	
Ab△sus2						
				Eb△sus		
Ab-△9	Bb 7b5b9			Eb△b9	Fb△#9	
Ab-△#11						

i MODE A HUNGARIAN MIN (1 2 b3 #4 5 b6 7)	II MODE B ORIENTAL (1 b2 3 4 b5 6 b7)	III MODE C IONIAN AUG #2 (1 #2 3 4 5 #6 7)	iv MODE D# LOCRIAN bb3 bb7 (1 b2 bb3 4 b5 b6 bb7)	V MODE E DOUBLE HARMONIC (1 b2 3 4 5 b6 7)	VI MODE F LYDIAN #6 #2 (1 #2 3 #4 5 #6 7)	vii MODE (1 b2 b3 b4 5 b6 bb7)
A^-	$B^{\flat 5}$	C^+		E	F	$G\#^-$
A^{SUS2}						
				E^{SUS}		
$A^{-\flat 6}$				$E^{\flat 6}$		$G\#^{-\flat 6}$
$A^{-\triangle}$	$B^{7\flat 5}$	$C^{\triangle +}$		$E^{\triangle}$	$F^{\triangle}$	
$A^{\triangle SUS2}$						
				$E^{\triangle SUS}$		
$A^{-\triangle 9}$	$B^{7\flat 5\flat 9}$			$E^{\triangle \flat 9}$	$F^{\triangle \# 9}$	
$A^{-\triangle \# 11}$						

i MODE Bb HUNGARIAN MIN (1 2 b3 #4 5 b6 7)	II MODE C ORIENTAL (1 b2 3 4 b5 6 b7)	III MODE Db IONIAN AUG #2 (1 #2 3 4 #5 6 7)	iv MODE E LOCRIAN bb3 bb7 (1 b2 bb3 4 b5 b6 bb7)	V MODE F DOUBLE HARMONIC (1 b2 3 4 5 b6 7)	VI MODE Gb LYDIAN #6 #2 (1 #2 3 #4 5 #6 7)	vii MODE (1 b2 b3 b4 5 b6 bb7)
$Bb-$	C^{b5}	Db^{+}		F	Gb	$A-$
$Bb^{SUS\,2}$						
				F^{SUS}		
$Bb-^{b6}$				F^{b6}		$A-^{b6}$
$Bb-^{\triangle}$	C^{7b5}	$Db^{\triangle+}$		$F^{\triangle}$	$Gb^{\triangle}$	
$Bb^{\triangle SUS\,2}$						
				$F^{\triangle SUS}$		
$Bb-^{\triangle 9}$	C^{7b5b9}			$F^{\triangle b9}$	$Gb^{\triangle \#9}$	
$Bb-^{\triangle \#11}$						

i MODE B HUNGARIAN MIN (1 2 b3 #4 5 b6 7)	II MODE C# ORIENTAL (1 b2 3 4 b5 6 b7)	III MODE D IONIAN AUG #2 (1 #2 3 4 #5 6 7)	iv MODE E# LOCRIAN bb3 bb7 (1 b2 bb3 4 b5 b6 bb7)	V MODE F# DOUBLE HARMONIC (1 2 3 4 5 b6 7)	VI MODE G LYDIAN #6 #2 (1 #2 3 #4 5 #6 7)	vii MODE (1 b2 b3 b4 5 b6 bb7)
$B-$	$C\#^{b5}$	D^+		$F\#$	G	$A\#-$
B^{sus2}						
				$F\#^{sus}$		
$B-^{b6}$				$F\#^{b6}$		$A\#-^{b6}$
$B-^{\triangle}$	$C\#^{7b5}$	$D^{\triangle+}$		$F\#^{\triangle}$	$G^{\triangle}$	
$B^{\triangle sus2}$						
				$F\#^{\triangle sus}$		
$B-^{\triangle 9}$	$C\#^{7b5b9}$			$F\#^{\triangle b9}$	$G^{\triangle\#9}$	
$B-^{\triangle\#11}$						

i MODE C HUNGARIAN MIN (1 2 b3 #4 5 b6 7)	II MODE D ORIENTAL (1 b2 3 4 b5 6 b7)	III MODE Eb IONIAN AUG #2 (1 #2 3 4 #5 6 7)	iv MODE F# LOCRIAN bb3 bb7 (1 b2 b3 4 b5 b6 bb7)	V MODE G DOUBLE HARMONIC (1 b2 3 4 5 b6 7)	VI MODE Ab LYDIAN #6 #2 (1 #2 3 #4 5 #6 7)	vii MODE (1 b2 b3 b4 5 b6 bb7)
C-	D^{b5}	Eb^{+}		G	Ab	B-
C^{sus2}						
				G^{sus}		
C-^{b6}				G^{b6}		B-^{b6}
C-$^{\triangle}$	D^{7b5}	Eb$^{\triangle+}$		G$^{\triangle}$	Ab$^{\triangle}$	
C$^{\triangle sus2}$						
				G$^{\triangle sus}$		
C-$^{\triangle 9}$	D^{7b5b9}			G$^{\triangle b9}$	Ab$^{\triangle \#9}$	
C-$^{\triangle \#11}$						

161

i MODE Db HUNGARIAN MIN (1 2 b3 #4 5 b6 7)	ii MODE Eb ORIENTAL (1 b2 3 4 b5 6 b7)	iii MODE Fb IONIAN AUG #2 (1 #2 3 4 #5 6 7)	iv MODE G LOCRIAN bb3 bb7 (1 b2 bb3 4 b5 b6 bb7)	V MODE Ab DOUBLE HARMONIC (1 b2 3 4 5 b6 7)	VI MODE Bbb LYDIAN #6 #2 (1 #2 3 #4 5 #6 7)	vii MODE (1 b2 b3 b4 5 b6 bb7)
Db-	Eb b5	Fb +		Ab	Bbb	C-
Db sus2						
				Ab sus		
Db-- b6				Ab b6		C-- b6
Db-△	Eb 7b5	Fb△+		Ab△	Bbb△	
Db△sus2						
				Ab△sus		
Db-△9	Eb 7b5b9			Ab△b9	Bbb△#9	
Db-△#11						

i MODE D HUNGARIAN MIN (1 2 b3 #4 5 b6 7)	II MODE E ORIENTAL (1 b2 3 4 b5 6 b7)	III MODE F IONIAN AUG #2 (1 #2 3 4 #5 6 7)	iv MODE G # LOCRIAN bb3 b7 (1 b2 b3 4 b5 b6 bb7)	V MODE A DOUBLE HARMONIC (1 b2 3 4 5 b6 7)	VI MODE Bb LYDIAN #6 #2 (1 #2 3 #4 5 #6 7)	vii MODE (1 b2 3 b4 5 b6 bb7)
D -	E b5	F +		A	Bb	C#-
D SUS 2						
				A SUS		
D -b6				A b6		C#-b6
D -△	E 7b5	F △+		A △	Bb△	
D △SUS 2						
				A △SUS		
D -△9	E 7b5b9			A △b9	Bb△#9	
D -△#11						

i MODE Eb HUNGARIAN MIN (1 2 b3 #4 5 b6 7)	II MODE F ORIENTAL (1 b2 3 4 b5 6 b7)	III MODE Gb IONIAN AUG #2 (1 #2 3 4 #5 6 7)	iv MODE A LOCRIAN bb3 bb7 (1 b2 b3 4 b5 b6 bb7)	V MODE Bb DOUBLE HARMONIC (1 b2 3 4 5 b6 7)	VI MODE Cb LYDIAN #6 #2 (1 #2 3 #4 5 #6 7)	vii MODE (1 b2 b3 4 5 b6 bb7)
$E\flat-$	$F^{\flat 5}$	$G\flat^{+}$		$B\flat$	$C\flat$	$D-$
$E\flat^{SUS2}$						
				$B\flat^{SUS}$		
$E\flat-^{\flat 6}$				$B\flat^{\flat 6}$		$D-^{\flat 6}$
$E\flat-^{\triangle}$	$F^{7\flat 5}$	$G\flat^{\triangle+}$		$B\flat^{\triangle}$	$C\flat^{\triangle}$	
$E\flat^{\triangle SUS2}$						
				$B\flat^{\triangle SUS}$		
$E\flat-^{\triangle 9}$	$F^{7\flat 5\flat 9}$			$B\flat^{\triangle\flat 9}$	$C\flat^{\triangle\#9}$	
$E\flat-^{\triangle\#11}$						

i MODE E HUNGARIAN MIN (1 2b 3 #4 5 b6 7)	II MODE F# ORIENTAL (1b 2 3 4b 5 6 b7)	III MODE G IONIAN AUG #2 (1 #2 3 4 #5 6 7)	iv MODE A# LOCRIAN bb3 bb7 (1 b2 bb3 4 b5 b6 bb7)	V MODE B DOUBLE HARMONIC (1 b2 3 4 5 b6 7)	VI MODE C LYDIAN #6 #2 (1 #2 3 #4 5 #6 7)	vii MODE (1b 2b 3b 4 5 b6bb7)
E -	F# ^{b5}	G $^{+}$		B	C	D# -
E $^{SUS\,2}$						
				B ^{SUS}		
E - ^{b6}				B ^{b6}		D# - ^{b6}
E - $^{\triangle}$	F# ^{7b5}	G $^{\triangle+}$		B $^{\triangle}$	C $^{\triangle}$	
E $^{\triangle SUS\,2}$						
				B $^{\triangle SUS}$		
E - $^{\triangle 9}$	F# ^{7b5b9}			B $^{\triangle b9}$	C $^{\triangle\#9}$	
E - $^{\triangle\#11}$						

THE HUNGARIAN MAJOR

I MODE - F HUNGARIAN MAJOR (1 #2 3 #4 5 6 ♭7)

BASIC TRIAD - F MAJOR (1 3 5)

F MAJOR SIXTH (1 3 5 6)

F SEVENTH (1 3 5 ♭7)

F SEVEN/SIXTH (1 3 5 6 ♭7)

F SHARP NINE (1 3 5 ♭7 #9)

ARPEGGIO OPTIONS

ii MODE
G#ALT♭♭6♮7 (1 ♭2 ♭3 4 ♭5 ♭♭6 ♮7)

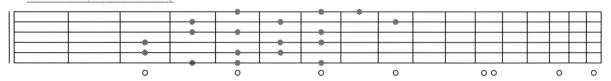

BASIC TRIAD G DIMINISHED (1 ♭3 ♭5)

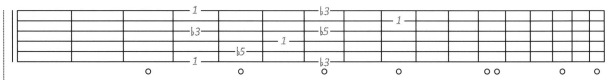

G DIMINISHED SEVENTH (1 ♭3 ♭5 ♭♭7)

ARPEGGIO OPTIONS

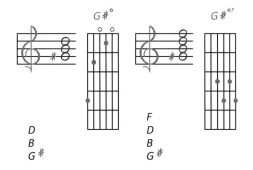

170

© 2009 BILL CRONKRITE

III MODE
A LOCRIAN ♮2 ♮7 (1 2 ♭3 4 ♭5 ♭6 7)

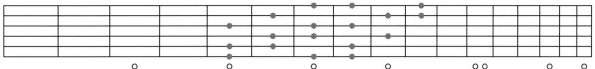

BASIC TRIAD A DIMINISHED (1 ♭3 ♭5)

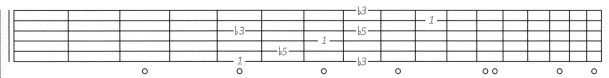

A MAJOR SEVENTH DIMINISHED (1 ♭3 ♭5 7)

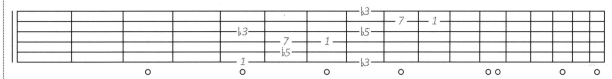

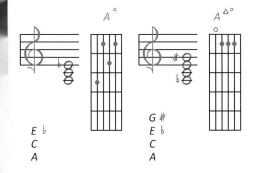

A °

A △°

E ♭
C
A

G ♯
E ♭
C
A

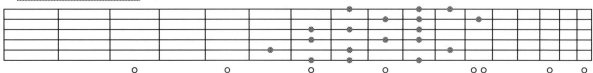

iv MODE
B ALT ♭6 (1 ♭2 ♭3 ♭4 ♭5 6 ♭7)

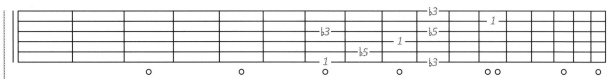

BASIC TRIAD B DIMINISHED (1 3 ♭♭5)♭

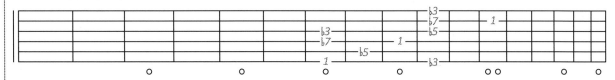

B HALF DIMINISHED (1 3♭ ♭5 7♭)

ARPEGGIO OPTIONS

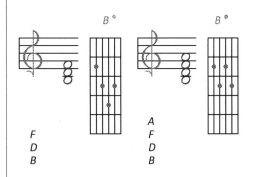

B °

F
D
B

A
F
D
B

172

v MODE
C MELODIC AUGMENTED (1 2 3♭4 ♯5♯6 7)

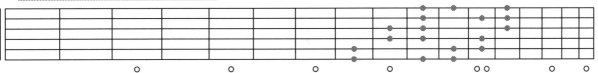

C MINOR MAJOR SEVENTH AUGMENTED (1 ♭3 ♭5 7♯)

ARPEGGIO OPTIONS

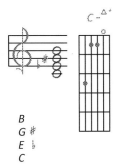

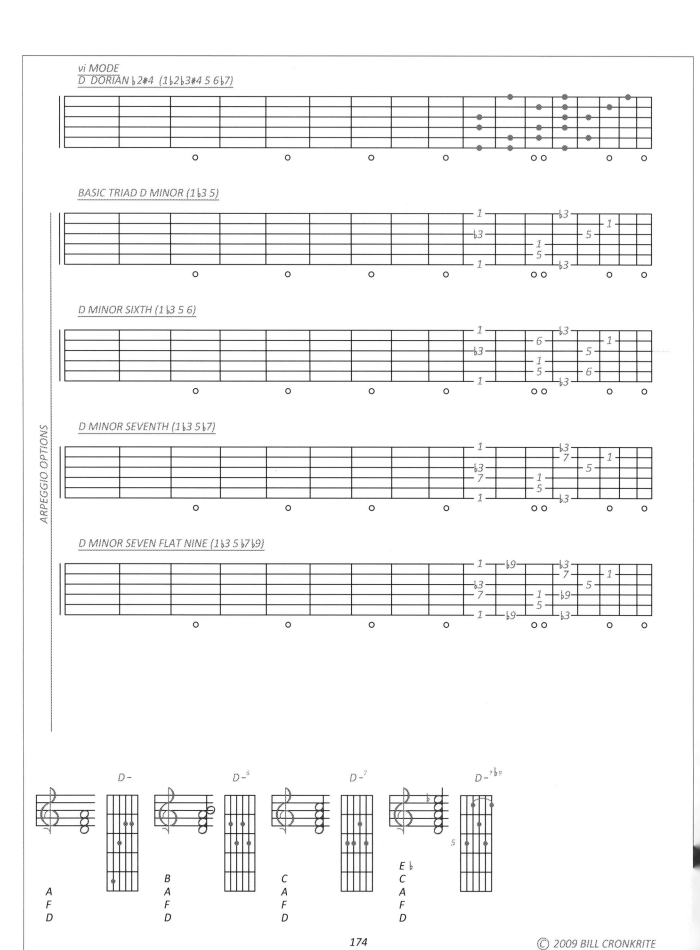

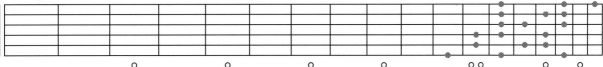

VII MODE
E♭ LYDIAN AUMENTED 3♯(1 2 3♯ 4♯ 5♯ 6 7)

THIS MODE HAS NO TRADITIONAL CHORD FORMS

Certainly there are chords that can be constructed to harmonize with this scale but the presence of the sharp in the third negates any traditional chord spellings or voicings.

I MODE F HUNGARIAN MAJ (1 #2 3 #4 5 6 b7)	ii MODE G# ALT b6 bb 7 (1 b2 b3 b4 b5 bb6 b7)	iii MODE A LOCRIAN ♮2 ♮7 (1 2 b3 4 b5 b6 7)	iv MODE B ALT ♮6 (1 b2 b3 ♮4 b5 6 b7)	v MODE C MELODIC AUGMENTED (1 2 b3 4 #5 6 7)	vi MODE D DORIAN b2 #4 (1 b2 b3 #4 5 6 b7)	VII MODE Eb LYDIAN AUGMENTED #3 (1 2 #3 #4 5 6 7)
F	G#°	A°	B°		D-	
F ^{6}					D- ^{6}	
F ^{7}	G# $^{°7}$	A $^{△°}$	B $^{∅}$	C- $^{△+}$	D- ^{7}	
F $^{7/6}$						
F $^{#9}$					D- ^{7b9}	

I MODE Gb HUNGARIAN MAJ (1 #2 3 #4 5 6 b7)	ii MODE A ALT b6 bb7 (1 b2 b3 4 b5 bb6 bb7)	iii MODE Bb LOCRIAN ♮2 ♮7 (1 2 b3 4 b5 b6 7)	iv MODE C ALT ♮6 (1 b2 b3 b4 b5 6 b7)	v MODE Db MELODIC AUGMENTED (1 2 b3 4 #5 6 7)	vi MODE Eb DORIAN b2 #4 (1 b2 b3 #4 5 6 b7)	VII MODE Fb LYDIAN AUGMENTED #3 (1 2 #3 #4 5 6 7)
Gb	A°	Bb°	C°		Eb-	
Gb⁶					Eb⁻⁶	
Gb▷⁷	A°⁷	Bb△°	C°	Db⁻△⁺	Eb⁻⁷	
Gb⁷ᐟ⁶						
Gb#⁹					Eb⁻⁷ᵇ⁹	

177

I MODE G HUNGARIAN MAJ (1 #2 3 #4 5 6 b7)	ii MODE A# ALT b6 b7 (1 b2 b3 4 b5 b6 b7)	iii MODE B LOCRIAN b2 b7 (1 2 b3 4 b5 b6 7)	iv MODE C# ALT b6 (1 b2 b3 b4 b5 6 b7)	v MODE D MELODIC AUGMENTED (1 2 b3 4 #5 6 7)	vi MODE E DORIAN b2 #4 (1 b2 b3 #4 5 6 b7)	VII MODE F LYDIAN AUGMENTED #3 (1 2 #3 #4 #5 6 7)
G	$A\#°$	$B°$	$C\#°$		$E-$	
G^6					$E-^6$	
G^7	$A\#^{°7}$	$B^{\triangle°}$	$C\#^{ø}$	$D-^{\triangle+}$	$E-^7$	
$G^{7/6}$						
$G^{\#9}$					$E-^{7b9}$	

I MODE Ab HUNGARIAN MAJ (1 *2 3 #4 5 6 b7)	ii MODE B ALT b6 bb7 (1 b2 b3 b4 b5 bb6 bb7)	iii MODE C LOCRIAN ♮2 ♮7 (1 2 b3 4 b5 b6 7)	iv MODE D ALT ♮6 (1 b2 b3 b4 b5 6 b7)	v MODE Eb MELODIC AUGMENTED (1 2 b3 4 #5 6 7)	vi MODE F DORIAN b2 #4 (1 b2 b3 #4 5 6 b7)	VII MODE Gb LYDIAN AUGMENTED #3 (1 2 #3 #4 #5 6 7)
Ab	B°	C°	D°		F-	
Ab^6					$F-^6$	
Ab^7	$B^{°7}$	$C^{△°}$	$D^{ø}$	$Eb-^{△+}$	$F-^7$	
$Ab^{7/6}$						
$Ab^{#9}$					$F-^{7b9}$	

I MODE A HUNGARIAN MAJ (1 #2 3 #4 5 6 b7)	ii MODE B# ALT b6 bb7 (1 b2 b3 b4 b5 b6 bb7)	iii MODE C# LOCRIAN ♮2 ♮7 (1 2 b3 4 b5 6 7)	iv MODE D# ALT ♮6 (1 b2 b3 ♮4 b5 6 b7)	v MODE E MELODIC AUGMENTED (1 2 b3 4 #5 6 7)	vi MODE F# DORIAN b2 #4 (1 b2 b3 #4 5 6 b7)	VII MODE G LYDIAN AUGMENTED #3 (1 2 #3 #4 5 6 7)
A	$B\#^{\circ}$	$C\#^{\circ}$	$D\#^{\circ}$		$F\#^{-}$	
A^{6}					$F\#^{-6}$	
A^{7}	$B\#^{\circ 7}$	$C\#^{\Delta \circ}$	$D\#^{\varnothing}$	$E^{-\Delta +}$	$F\#^{-7}$	
$A^{7/6}$						
$A^{\#9}$					$F\#^{-7b9}$	

I MODE Bb HUNGARIAN MAJ (1 ♯2 3 ♯4 5 6 ♭7)	ii MODE C♯ ALT ♭♭6 ♭♭7 (1 ♭2 ♭3 ♭4 ♭5 ♭♭6 ♭♭7)	iii MODE D LOCRIAN ♮2 ♮7 (1 2 ♭3 4 ♭5 6 ♭7)	iv MODE E ALT ♮6 (1 ♭2 ♭3 ♭4 ♭5 6 ♭7)	v MODE F MELODIC AUGMENTED (1 2 ♭3 4 ♯5 6 7)	vi MODE G DORIAN ♭2 ♯4 (1 ♭2 ♭3 ♯4 5 6 ♭7)	VII MODE Ab LYDIAN AUGMENTED ♯3 (1 2 ♯3 ♯4 ♯5 6 7)
Bb	$C\#°$	$D°$	$E°$		$G\text{-}$	
$Bb^{\text{-}6}$					$G^{\text{-}6}$	
$Bb^{\text{-}7}$	$C\#^{°7}$	$D^{\triangle°}$	$E^{ø}$	$F^{\text{-}\triangle+}$	$G^{\text{-}7}$	
$Bb^{\text{-}7/6}$						
$Bb^{\#9}$					$G^{\text{-}7b9}$	

I MODE B HUNGARIAN MAJ (1 #2 3 #4 5 6 b7)	ii MODE C## ALT b6 bb7 (1 b2 b3 b4 b5 bb6 bb7)	iii MODE D# LOCRIAN ♮2 ♮7 (1 2 b3 4 b5 b6 7)	iv MODE E# ALT ♮6 (1 b2 b3 b4 b5 6 b7)	v MODE F# MELODIC AUGMENTED (1 2 b3 4 #5 6 7)	vi MODE G# DORIAN b2 #4 (1 b2 b3 #4 5 6 b7)	VII MODE A LYDIAN AUGMENTED #3 (1 2 #3 #4 #5 6 7)
B	$C\#\#°$	$D\#°$	$E\#°$		$G\#{-}$	
B^6					$G\#{-}^5$	
B^7	$C\#\#°^7$	$D\#^{\Delta°}$	$E\#^{ø}$	$F\#{-}^{\Delta+}$	$G\#{-}^7$	
$B^{7/6}$						
$B^{\#9}$					$G\#{-}^{7b9}$	

I MODE C HUNGARIAN MAJ (1 #2 3 #4 5 6 b7)	ii MODE D# ALT bb6 bb7 (1 b2 b3 b4 b5 bb6 b7)	iii MODE E LOCRIAN ♮2 ♮7 (1 2 b3 4 b5 b6 7)	iv MODE F# ALT ♮6 (1 b2 b3 b4 b5 6 b7)	v MODE G MELODIC AUGMENTED (1 2 b3 4 #5 6 7)	vi MODE A DORIAN b2 #4 (1 b2 b3 #4 5 6 b7)	VII MODE Bb LYDIAN AUGMENTED #3 (1 2 #3 #4 #5 6 7)
C	D# °	E °	F# °		A-	
C ^{5}					A- ^{6}	
C ^{7}	D# $^{°7}$	E $^{Δ°}$	F# $^{°}$	G- $^{Δ+}$	A- ^{7}	
C $^{7/6}$						
C $^{#9}$					A- ^{7b9}	

I MODE Db HUNGARIAN MAJ (1 #2 3 #4 5 6 b7)	ii MODE E ALT b6 bb7 (1 b2 b3 b4 b5 b6 bb7)	iii MODE F LOCRIAN ♮2 ♮7 (1 2 b3 4 b5 b6 7)	iv MODE G ALT ♮6 (1 b2 b3 b4 b5 6 b7)	v MODE Ab MELODIC AUGMENTED (1 2 b3 4 #5 6 7)	vi MODE Bb DORIAN b2 #4 (1 b2 b3 #4 5 6 b7)	VII MODE Cb LYDIAN AUGMENTED #3 (1 2 #3 #4 5 6 7)
Db	E °	F °	G °		Bb-	
Db⁶					Bb-⁶	
Db⁷	E °⁷	F Δ°	G ⌀	Ab-Δ+	Bb-⁷	
Db⁷/⁶						
Db#⁹					Bb-⁷b⁹	

I MODE D HUNGARIAN MAJ (1 #2 3 #4 5 6 b7)	ii MODE E# ALT b6 b7 (1 b2 b3 b4 b5 bb6 b7)	iii MODE F# LOCRIAN ♮2 ♮7 (1 2 b3 4 b5 b6 7)	iv MODE G# ALT ♮6 (1 b2 b3 b4 b5 6 b7)	v MODE A MELODIC AUGMENTED (1 2 b3 4 #5 6 7)	vi MODE B DORIAN b2 #4 (1 b2 b3 #4 5 6 b7)	VII MODE C LYDIAN AUGMENTED #3 (1 2 #3 #4 5 6 7)
D	$E\#^{\circ}$	$F\#^{\circ}$	$G\#^{\circ}$		$B-$	
D^{6}					$B-^{6}$	
D^{7}	$E\#^{\circ 7}$	$F\#^{\Delta\circ}$	$G\#^{\emptyset}$	$A-^{\Delta+}$	$B-^{7}$	
$D^{7/6}$						
$D^{\#9}$					$B-^{7b9}$	

I MODE Eb HUNGARIAN MAJ (1 #2 3 #4 5 6 b7)	ii MODE F# ALT b6 bb7 (1 b2 b3 4 b5 bb6 bb7)	iii MODE G LOCRIAN b2 b7 (1 2 b3 4 b5 b6 7)	iv MODE A ALT b6 (1 b2 b3 b4 b5 6 b7)	v MODE Bb MELODIC AUGMENTED (1 2 b3 4 #5 6 7)	vi MODE C DORIAN b2 #4 (1 b2 b3 #4 5 6 b7)	VII MODE Db LYDIAN AUGMENTED #3 (1 2 #3 #4 5 6 7)
Eb	F#°	G°	A°		C-	
Eb⁶					C-⁶	
Eb⁷	F#°⁷	G Δ°	A ⌀	Bb-Δ⁺	C-⁷	
Eb⁷ᐟ⁶						
Eb#⁹					C-⁷ᵇ⁹	

186

I MODE E HUNGARIAN MAJ ($1\,\sharp2\,3\,\sharp4\,5\,6\,\flat7$)	ii MODE F##ALT $\flat6\,\flat\flat7$ ($1\,\flat2\,\flat3\,\flat4\,\flat5\,\flat6\,\flat7$)	iii MODE G# LOCRIAN $\natural2\,\natural7$ ($1\,2\,\flat3\,4\,\flat5\,\flat6\,7$)	iv MODE A# ALT $\natural6$ ($1\,\flat2\,\flat3\,\flat4\,\flat5\,6\,\flat7$)	v MODE B MELODIC AUGMENTED ($1\,2\,\flat3\,\sharp4\,5\,6\,7$)	vi MODE C# DORIAN $\flat2\,\sharp4$ ($1\,\flat2\,\flat3\,\sharp4\,5\,6\,\flat7$)	VII MODE D LYDIAN AUGMENTED #3 ($1\,2\,\sharp3\,\sharp4\,5\,6\,7$)
E	$F\sharp\sharp°$	$G\sharp°$	$A\sharp°$		$C\sharp{-}$	
E^6					$C\sharp{-}^6$	
E^7	$F\sharp\sharp°^7$	$G\sharp^{\Delta°}$	$A\sharp^{ø}$	$B{-}^{\Delta+}$	$C\sharp{-}^7$	
$E^{7/6}$						
$E^{\sharp9}$					$C\sharp{-}^{7\flat9}$	

Printed in the United States
by Baker & Taylor Publisher Services